Ida Jo Pajunen
Master's degree i. Cambridge and another Master's degree in traditions of yoga and meditation from the School of Oriental and African Studies (SOAS), University of London. She was awarded the title of Yoga Acharya (Master of Yoga) by the Sivananda Yoga Vedanta Centre. She is the co-author of several Ghosh Yoga Practice Manuals and has edited and published historic manuscripts. She makes her home in Minnesota, USA, but travels all over the world to teach practical yoga, history and philosophy, and to perform music. She is a lifelong and award-winning violinist and vocalist.

Connect with her
@ghoshyoga @idajomusic
www.ghoshyoga.org

STRONG WOMAN
REBA RAKSHIT

The Life and Times of a Stuntmaster

Ida Jo Pajunen

Om Books International

First published in 2024 by

Om Books International

Corporate & Editorial Office
A-12, Sector 64, Noida 201 301
Uttar Pradesh, India
Phone: +91 120 477 4100
Email: editorial@ombooks.com
Website: www.ombooksinternational.com

Sales Office
107, Ansari Road, Darya Ganj,
New Delhi 110 002, India
Phone: +91 11 4000 9000
Email: sales@ombooks.com
Website: www.ombooks.com

Copyright © Ida Jo Pajunen 2024

ALL RIGHTS RESERVED. The views and opinions expressed in this book are those of the author, and have been verified to the extent possible, and the publishers are in no way liable for the same. No part of this book may be reproduced or transmitted in any form by any means, electronic or mechanical, including photocopying and recording, or by any information storage and retrieval system, except as may be expressly permitted in writing by the publisher.

ISBN: 978-93-5376-960-4

Printed in India

10 9 8 7 6 5 4 3 2 1

To
All the strong women

Contents

Author's Note   xi
Prologue   xiii

From Comilla to Calcutta—a Journey of Self-discovery for Young Reba

1. Anima—the Wild Child   3
   Serious about Explorations And Adventures

2. Becoming Reba—the Lucky One   10
   'It Is Not Possible for a Bird to Fly with Only One Wing'

3. Calcutta—the New Home   18
   A World Away from Comilla

4. Bengal in the Aftermath of Hindu Renaissance   26
   An Era of Viewing Traditions through the Lens of Reason And Logic

Post-Independence India—a Nation on the Churn

5. Reba Joins the Movement of Body,
    Spirit And Country   33
    An Attempt to Build Indian Identity
    through Bodily Purity

6. Finding Her Guru—Bishnu Charan Ghosh   47
    A Journey from Darkness to Light

7. Bishnu Charan Ghosh—the Making of a Legend   59
    How the Leading Exponent of Yoga Changed Lives

8. Fractured Freedom for India—the Partition of 1947   69
    More Independence for Its Women

Ghosh And Reba—Building a Relationship

9. Bishnu Charan Ghosh's Star Pupils   79
    'The Guru Is the Father, the Guru Is the Mother,
    the Guru Is God'

10. Reba—the New Woman   83
    Becoming Strong in a Focused, Calm Way

11. Passing the Test with Flying Colours   96
    How Reba Mastered Her Breath Control

12. Reba the Star Is Born   108
    The World Had Never Seen Anyone Like Her Before

Stuntmaster Reba—a Class Act

13. 'I Felt Nothing At All' 125
 How Reba Felt When a Baby Elephant Walked over Her

14. The Show-stopper, the Guru And the Act 136
 A Remarkable Feat of Strength, Beauty, Charisma And Skill

15. The Show Never Stops ... 151
 The Day It Almost Did

16. Fighting Hate, Malice And Violence with Aplomb 160
 The Pride of Bengal under Threat

'Circus Beauty Queen' Reba—Wearing a Crown of Thorns

17. Shows, Travel, Sleep 173
 Did Reba Fully Belong to Herself?

18. Would Ghosh's Experiment Succeed? 184
 Mastering the Art of Survival

19. Circus, Yoga And Magic—Intertwined Together 196
 Reba at the P.C. Sorcar Show

20. The Final Bow 205
 Reba Sets the Barbell Down

Epilogue	211
Present Day	
Afterword	215
Acknowledgements	217

Author's Note

This is a true story.

I have researched for this book by reading a short essay written by Reba Rakshit, interviewing her family and those who knew her, and going through articles or advertisements that mentioned her.

I have added extensively researched sections to provide insights into the time and place, along with the social and political discussions prevalent during Reba's life. I have refrained from repeating what I believe to be fabrications about her life, though you may hear them elsewhere. These details are not accolades I have missed, rather what I believe to have been embellished for the sake of her promotion.

I have attempted to hold true to the time in which Reba lived, while at times embracing the perspective history can offer.

Some of the dialogues in the book are reconstructed from my interviews or video recordings that feature someone other than Reba performing the same stunts Reba described. The notes provide more details.

I have tried my utmost to make this book as accurate as possible. I hope you enjoy Reba's story as much as I enjoyed writing it.

Prologue

Calcutta 1957

The evening came alive as the crowds drew near to the circus tent. Outside the big top, whose yellow-and-red canvas towered over the park, people were gathering in huge numbers and pressing towards the entrance. Some had come from villages far, far away just for the night's show. Back home in their village, they had seen the smaller circus acts—a little girl walking on the tightrope under the fiery sun. They had squinted, looking up at the sky to watch her balance on the thin wire while she had walked back and forth, as if on air, her rough young feet gripping the tightrope while the jingle-jangle of her bangles sounded in the wind. They had heard unbelievable stories of what they might see if they came to the great circus in the city. 'The tightrope act is nothing compared to what you will see in the big ring!' So, they had saved their money to travel to the city—by train, by bus, by foot. They were promised the greatest sight to behold, the biggest act in the biggest ring.

The city people came too. This was not a show that could be missed. The newspapers in both English and Bengali ran advertisement after advertisement promising the 'rare thrill of your life-time'.[1] Anticipation had drenched Calcutta from Maniktala to Alipore; the word of what was to come spread far and wide. Now winter was finally here, and they were waiting in anticipation for the finale of the circus act.

As the crowd shuffled towards the entrance, shoulder to shoulder, they muttered anxiously to the strangers standing nearby: 'Can you believe that it is true? An elephant! She takes it on her chest! A woman! Has anyone ever done it before?!'

Outside the tent, an orchestra filled the air with loud, happy music of the love song '*O leke pehla pehla pyar*' from the blockbuster movie *CID*. The cheerful rhythm backed the evening's excitement in a rhythmic pulse. Swarms of people moved in murmuration around the tent, waiting for their turn to get in. Young girls and boys ran barefoot on the grass. Weaving unnoticed among the adults, they pushed against each other for a chance to get close to the massive tent and peer through its openings. The children with their torn clothes and dirty faces would not get to see the show from the inside. But those small enough to look through the pinholes in the canvas would try for a glance.

Excitement coursed through the veins of everyone there. For those outside the tent, slowly making their way in, the anticipation was overwhelming. Exhausted from the nags of daily life, they were ready to see something out of the ordinary. Something breathtaking. Remarkable. Spectacular.

---

[1] Classified Ad 18. No Title. (1 November 1957). *The Times of India* (1861–2010).

The excitement was different backstage. The performers paced back and forth, feeling both anxious and familiar. This feeling of excitement was not so much because of the chance to *escape* from life—as it was for the crowd outside—but more because of the *risk* to their lives. Most of their acts were inherently dangerous in some way, risking injury or even death if something went wrong. It was not sheer panic that the performers felt because they were the *stars*. The eyes of the crowd stayed glued on them. When the performers took the ring, they could revel in the fact that they were the reason everyone was there. They were the reason the crowd clenched their fists in anticipation, gasped, held their breath and erupted into awe-filled praise. After all, it was that very danger which made the circus a spectacle so many flocked to see.

Backstage, Reba prepared.

She carefully dressed herself in white. The shiny, tight fabric hugged the curves of her tall and slender frame. She worked to arrange the fabric just so. She pulled the delicately tailored leotard up around her body until the straps rested on her slender shoulders. She quickly slipped her toes into her sandals, which were bejewelled in beads and sequins, and slicked down her ebony hair. Once her costume was arranged and her hair fixed, she stood still.

It was always hard to tell whether it was calmness or numbness she was feeling. She had trained her mind for *ekagrata*, to be one-pointed, to withstand and bypass tension, anxiety or stress. But numbness always had a way of finding her. As danger approached, a dense haze would engulf her. She would lose track of reality for a few moments before emerging on the other side, unfazed.

Near her was Bishnu Charan Ghosh, her guru and confidant. That night, he was dressed in a black suit and a pair of shiny black shoes, his short, muscular body filling out his stylish clothes. He was the best-dressed man backstage—he was there to look after Reba, project professionalism and command the performance. He buzzed around with aggressive determination, alternating between selling the act that Reba was about to perform and cutting deals for ideas he had in the works. He was a showman; a smooth talker with a very convincing way about him. In between conversations, he would circle back to Reba, gesturing a firm *shanto hao* (stay calm) in her direction.

In a clear voice, she would reply, '*Chinta korben na. Bhalo achhi* (Don't worry. I am fine.).'[2]

Ghosh had already climbed his way up in society and rubbed shoulders with socialites and celebrities. He was a household name with a bustling *akhara* and yoga centre that bore his name. His students went far in life and it was a testament to his training, showmanship and sheer determination. But success in the performance ring would not sustain itself. It took constant feeding with new talent, harder acts and grander feats of strength. Furthermore, the world's entertainment arena was transitioning from stage to screen, so he was constantly juggling innovation, both the world's and his own. How did it all fit together? What was the best way to secure stardom? He took it upon himself to ensure that he held sufficient rank in society, despite the fact that the stars he had a hand in creating, like Reba herself, were the ones

---

[2] This brief dialogue is reconstructed from a performance by Bishnu Ghosh's daughter, Karuna Ghosh, who later performed elephant lifting.

actually standing in the ring, performing the acts in front of thousands of people.

As Reba prepared to perform her act, she heard his voice behind her, talking in the direction of anyone who would listen, 'It's a very dangerous act!'

His deep tone cut through the bustle.

'Tonight the great performer, my star pupil, Reba Rakshit will perform the stunt. The finale act! The greatest stunt there ever was!'

As she listened to him describe the danger of what she was about to do, the familiar feeling of excitement tinged with panic furiously ran through her veins. What she was about to do was a mix of yogic skill and pure showmanship. Whether or not it succeeded—as it had so many times before—would be a matter of careful execution … and the grace of God.

Each time she performed the stunt she was afraid, but by this point her life had been turned over to the higher beings many times. She often felt she was living on borrowed time. She had come close to death a few times already due to stunts gone wrong. If this was her time to go, so be it. So many around her had fallen fatally ill; or worse, died from the traumas that years of war, nationalism and cultural change had brought. So, she prepared herself for the act. If she were to miscalculate the subtle timing of the stunt, and if it were to claim her very life, she prayed only that it would not happen *that night*.

Because her sister Jyotsna and young nephew Swapan were coming to watch the show. Usually she could bear the thought of the act going wrong as she knew the risk. But she could not bear the thought of it happening before Swapan. If that were to happen, the horror of watching his *mashi* crushed to death would be etched in his memory for decades to come. The sound of bones crushed to dust, the sight of Reba's flattened chest and limp limbs would haunt him forever.

Reba set out to make a deal with the universe. Under her breath, muffled by her Bishtuda's commanding voice behind her and the cacophony of musical instruments and voices outside the tent, she murmured, '*Ektu aj rate na* (please not tonight).'

In all corners of the arena backstage, others were preparing to take the stage in turn. Animals and people alike. As the elephants stood chewing on piles of hay, the horses were fitted with their jewelled harnesses. Their coats shone a brilliant bay, even as their ribs rippled up against their skin.

Fearless Madhavi leaned her back against a steel cage as three Bengal tigers growled behind the bars. Radha dressed and prepared her act: The Revolving Knife Throw. Shankaran and Lilly were stretching their spines up and back, then draping their arms to the floor, limbering up in time to fly through the air in their Springboard act. The flying trapeze star himself, Mukundan, praised as the 'perfect mix of brains and brawn', slipped on his boots and fringed vest. The whole troupe would be ready just in time for the immense crowd to finish filing in.[3]

As the crowd gathered under the striped tent, Jyotsna pushed to get to the front, grasping the hand of her son Swapan. They caught the eyes of Ghosh as he determinedly paced back and forth.

'*Esho*! *Esho*! (Come! Come!)!' he said loudly, gesturing for them to come closer. His clear and loud voice cut through the noise. The sea of people between them and the stage slowly

---

[3] Greatest Show on Earth. Kamala Circus Souvenir Programme. 1956. Open access.

parted, creating an opening just wide enough for Jyotsna and little Swapan to squeeze through and make their way closer to the front. Swapan, clenching his mother's hand, was easily swallowed up by the crowd. If it weren't for Ghosh's command, Swapan would have only heard the performance. He would have only been able to judge the performance by the rhythms of tense silence pierced by the gasps of the crowd. Now he had a front-row view, he kept his eyes glued to the stage.

The voice of the Master of Ceremonies boomed through the tent: 'Ladies and gentlemen, boys and girls!'

The show was beginning.

The lights over the crowd lowered and all eyes turned to the stage. Reba stood behind the curtain, dressed and ready, but she had to wait until the final act. She would not go on until the end. This gave Jyotsna and Swapan time to relax and enjoy the show, pushing back their trepidation until later in the evening.

Every performance of her talented colleagues was just a warm-up act for the finale. For *her*. Her act was the one the circus owners could not live without, the one they wrote about in the papers, the one that brought the large audiences no matter which city the circus was in.

As the evening passed and each act was punctuated by cheers and applause from the audience, the finale drew near. The crowd stood ready, its anticipation building. Expectation would soon meet reality.

Finally, the Master of Ceremonies walked dramatically into the centre of the ring. The crowd fell silent. He opened his arms wide and proclaimed, 'Now, the moment you have all been waiting for!'

Jyotsna was speechless, her breath caught in her chest while the rest of the crowd cheered Reba into the circus ring. Jyotsna desperately hoped Reba would live up to her name. *Reba* meaning *lucky*.

As Jyotsna stood with her son's hand in hers, she thought of her baby sister. She knew her as little Anima Rakshit, long before the world knew her as Reba. She had been a brave and wild-hearted girl, unaware of all that life would thrust upon her.

Jyotsna was brought back into the moment as the Master of Ceremonies continued, 'The great Reba Rakshit …'

Jyotsna and Swapan stood taller now with their eyes wide.

'The great Reba Rakshit will defy death …' the Master of Ceremonies continued. Jyotsna sharply inhaled, calming the nervous waves pulsing through her body.

Ghosh stood proud and assured. Everyone's eyes were on his star pupil.

As Reba walked to the centre of the ring, the Master of Ceremonies continued, his words drawn out as the cheers from the crowd grew louder and louder, 'The great Reba Rakshit will defy death by lifting an elephant on her chest!'[4]

---

[4] Classified Ad 18. No Title. (1 November 1957). *The Times of India* (1861–2010).

From Comilla to Calcutta—a Journey of Self-discovery for Young Reba

1

Anima—the Wild Child

Serious about Explorations And Adventures

Anima Rakshit lived the first decade of her life in Comilla, on the eastern edge of undivided India in modern Bangladesh. To her, it was as if she lived on the edge of the world. Even as a very young girl, Anima loved the natural world—the forest, the rivers and the wild animals. She never missed an opportunity to escape from her house into the nearby patches of wilderness. Her adventurous and mischievous nature drew her away from the tidy structures of her surroundings, towards the chaotic beauty of the outdoors, where no one could tell her '*koro na* (don't do that)'. In the wild, with the forest towering over her and the rivers running through, she was certain that the world was filled with beings and powers far greater than her.[1]

---

[1] Reba Rakshit, 'The Sport of Elephant Lifting', in *Kamalasundari*, eds Jayita Bagchi and Sumeru Mukhopadhyay (Kolkata: Lyriqal Books,

One morning, Anima roamed freely through the nearby sal forest. She woke up at dawn, her sleep pierced as the Goddess of Dawn Usha slowly illuminated her room. She liked to venture into the forest while the day was new, the ground was still damp and cool, and the sun's golden light streamed through the branches. As she skipped and ran through the trees, she could feel the presence of the goddess with the warm sun touching her skin. Anima's breath quickened as she began to run, lengthening her strides, her long slender limbs reaching through the air. Finally, when she was deep in the forest, she stopped and looked around. *Which tree is the tallest?* she wondered, gazing up high. She chose carefully, making sure she found the one that reached all the way up to the sky. Then she wrapped her thin arms and legs around its trunk, hugging it tightly. With her face pressed against the wood she could smell the dank bark, somewhere between growth and decay, the smell of life and death intertwined. She wiggled hard, lifting one arm up and then the other, slowly climbing her way up as high as she could, the bark scraping her soft skin. She rose above the earth, the wild animals, the people until she could feel the wind. She was not afraid; she was fearless.

There were so many wild creatures to look out for—snakes, jackals, foxes, bears, sambar deer; sometimes Anima would even catch a glimpse of the Royal Bengal tiger. She often wondered, *What would it be like being powerful; so striking? What would it be like being the object of such attention and praise?*

Then there were the elephants.

2018), 253–264. This essay was written by Reba, but the volume was published in 2018. I was unable to find out who submitted the essay for publication in this collection, or when exactly Reba wrote it.

According to a legend, elephants once had wings. Despite their massive size, they flew so high that they mated with the clouds. One day, a few elephants were sitting high in a tree, resting while they split their time between earth and sky. Under the tree, beneath the elephants, a holy man was sitting with his students, teaching them a lesson. As he went on teaching, the heft of the elephants' bodies caused a tree branch to break and fall to the ground along with an elephant. When the elephant fell, it killed some of the students. The holy man was furious. He immediately went to the gods and demanded that they remove the elephants' wings as punishment. The gods agreed and the elephants' wings disappeared, dooming them to live their entire lives walking the earth. However, since the elephants had grown close to the clouds, they could ask for rain any time the earth needed it. Thus, they were the beings called upon to end a drought.[2] The peaceful giants towered above nearly everyone else, but they never frightened little Anima.

After running in the forest and climbing trees, Anima swam in the lake. First she floated on her back on the water's surface, touched on all sides by the gentle ripples, cooling her off from the day's growing heat. Whether she was sitting high on a tree branch, running through the woods or floating in the water, Anima's imagination ran like a tiger, taking over her mind and devouring her thoughts. She had the imagination of any child, with an adventurous nature unique to her.

Once her skin felt cool, she flipped onto her belly and worked on her swimming strokes. She reached an arm

---

[2] Karl Gröning and Martin Saller, *Elephants: A Cultural and Natural History* (Cologne: Konemann Publishing, 1999), 124.

overhead, scooped the water with her hand and pulled it quickly down to her side. She repeated this motion over and over, perfecting its rhythm.

Reach, scoop, pull. Reach, scoop, pull.

As her body settled into the pattern, her mind drifted to another time and place. Suddenly, she was no longer a child swimming for fun—now she was racing, racing to win. She refined each kick and stroke in order to shoot through the water at top speed. She wanted, *needed* to *win*, even if the race was only in her imagination and against herself. Her siblings were not interested in athletics or adventure, so Anima had to push against herself, trying to be better, faster and faster. Skimming through the water, she measured her breath just so, matching inhalation and exhalation. She timed the lifting of her head to be just so, in order to get a mouthful of air, not water. *Timing is key*, she knew. *Breathing must be perfect.* If she took a breath at the wrong moment, she would choke. One moment off and she could drown. While swimming, she realized the great importance of the breath.

Once she was satisfied that the race was won and her limbs were overtaken by sheer exhaustion, Anima stopped swimming and floated again on her back in the glistening waters of the pond, underneath the endless sky and surrounded by the vastness of India and the infinite.

When Anima returned home, her elder sister Jyotsna was cutting potatoes; her three little brothers were playing about, running here and there; and her father was waiting for her to return. His face wore a thoughtful frown. Anima knew that he worried about her, always saying that she should be more serious and try to be womanly. *But I am serious,* she thought, *serious about explorations and adventures*!

Upendra Chandra Rakshit was not a tall man, but he stood upright and proud. His hair was combed neatly, emphasizing his often serious expression. He wore a white short-sleeved button-down shirt with big pockets on the front. His lips were pressed together in a look somewhere between thoughtfulness and frustration. 'Anima,' he said as she stood in front of him, still dripping from her swim, 'you must study and learn how to keep a home. You will be married soon. Cook with Jyotsna instead of running around outside.'

In the eyes of her father, there was only one path forward for a woman—that of the hearth and home. Young girls became wives and then mothers. Jyotsna was on that path already.

'But, Baba, *look*! I am getting strong! And every day, I am getting faster!' She held her arms out to the side, bent the elbows and squeezed her muscles for him to see. She had seen the bodybuilders at a Durga Puja programme show off their big muscles like this. Her limbs though tough and strong were skinny, and not as impressive as she hoped for. She barely stood half of her father's height, but she looked at him in the eye and pleaded, desperate to convince him that the mornings spent in the forest and lake were worth every moment.

'Nonsense, Anima,' he shook his head with growing impatience. 'Each of us has a role to play. I go to work at the insurance company.[3] Why? To take care of this family. You too have to learn to do your part.'

With that said, he crossed his arms in front of his chest. There was no argument she could make to change his mind. He saw the world the way he saw it.

---

[3] Rakshit, 'The Sport of Elephant Lifting', 253–264.

Anima's mother, on the other hand, was different. Despite being from an era when a woman's place was to be a wife, a mother and a caretaker, Suhasini Rakshit was progressive and wanted her children to be brave and liberated from social and political binds. It was the 1930s, and the world was changing rapidly, especially for women. She liked the fact that her little Anima was bold and daring, independent and a little wild; that she returned from her morning adventures with arms and legs covered in scrapes, clothes marked with dirt and hair still dripping wet. Suhasini never said a word to detract from Anima's unusual interests, instead she encouraged her daughter to pursue her interests and dreams, no matter how impossible. She knew things would be different for Anima, since she was born in a different time.

In ancient times, a woman's life was often not hers to live at all. Maintaining the social order was most important back then, and this meant that women were held in low social status.[4] Of course, there are legends of a few famous and important women who are remembered by history, but endless stories of men easily overshadow them. There are many powerful goddesses worshipped by the people but that did not give ordinary women any voice or power. The society was split according to caste and gender, with women assigned to the bottom rung.

However, the times were changing. New possibilities were beginning to appear for the *matir meye*, the daughters of the soil. Now girls could be educated outside of their home, though this was much more common for boys. Modern women could

---

[4] 'Women in Hinduism'. Oxford Centre for Hindu Studies Online. Section 3. https://ochsonline.org/course/women-in-hinduism/

earn a living, though they were not allowed to keep it as their own, or own property. Much of the shift towards educating women in the past few decades seemed motivated by freeing India from British oppression. The men of India needed women to be smart and strong to join the movement for Independence. But the reason really did not matter. Education was valuable, and once it was extended to the daughters, it could not be taken away. Maybe it took colonial oppression to create the opportunity for formal women's education. Time, karma and the gods all work in mysterious ways. Suhasini was an ardent devotee of Ramakrishna Paramahamsa[5] and his disciple Swami Vivekananda.

She brought the spiritual ideals of Ramakrishna into their home. Ancient ideas were influencing modern society, and modern society was reshaping tradition. Time flows like the current of a river, never stopping. Whenever the current hits a rock in the river bed, it simply bends around it adjusting its flow, but always moves forward. As Anima began to help her sister Jyotsna in the kitchen, she thought to herself, *OK, I'll learn to cook, but never at the expense of my adventures.*

---

[5] 'Elephant Girl', *The Times of India* (15 April 2001), B7.

2

Becoming Reba—the Lucky One

'It Is Not Possible for a Bird to Fly with Only One Wing'

All around Anima were stories about her home, the land, culture and the beliefs that made people who they were. They lived in *parbata*, *nadi*, *samudra* and *devlok*; the mountains which have names, the rivers full of power, the ocean to which everything flows in time and the spirits who animated it all. Anima with her wild streak, love of nature, and grand imagination loved tales and legends. The legends and beliefs lived in the heart of the people and in the heart of the land.

The great land of India housed both the ordinary and the extraordinary. Even the name Comilla, which means pond of the lotus, was balanced on the edge between the natural and the divine worlds. It was named for both the lotus flower which floats on the water, and Goddess Lakshmi, who brings fertility and prosperity.

Every time Anima ran through the forest or climbed up a tree and into the sky, she too was somewhere between the nature and the spirit; as if everyone is part of their country, its people, the infinite.

'How long ago was the ancient time?' Anima asked her mother in order to grasp the vastness of space and time.

'Think of your *didima*,' Suhasini replied. 'She is my mother, and then think of her mother and her mother. Imagine one hundred mothers of mothers. Then one hundred more.'

Anima's imagination ran wild. She had visions of hundreds of white-haired, old women who appeared fragile, yet carried each other on their backs, each mother caring for her daughter and all of those who came after.

As *time* took shape in her mind, she wondered about *space*.

The Indus and the Ganga, and their many tributaries, provided food and water for countless generations of mothers and daughters, fathers and sons.

The coastal regions, though susceptible to temperamental seas, could harness the monsoon winds for sailing ships and other maritime purposes. The Sundarbans and other estuaries lie far to the east of India in the Ganges Delta, though not quite as far east as Comilla. They provided ports, helpful for sustaining human life. For two thousand years, the eastern shore supported trade with south-east Asia and China. This trade included not only crops and goods, but also ideas. Even Buddhism took shape as it travelled along this route.[6]

Suhasini would remind Anima of the sacredness of the place.

'Great spiritual sages lived here, in this very land,' she would remind Anima. 'Some still do.'

---

[6] Romila Thapar, *Early India: From the Origins to AD 1300* (Gurugram: Penguin Books India, 2015), 47.

Anima thought about this as her mother continued.

'The spirits of the sages are always alive and with us. But enlightened ones walk among us even today. They are here to teach us the way.'

One night after the usual argument with her father about her future, Anima was confused by his incessant demands.

Suhasini explained to Anima, 'It is tradition for a girl to marry and become a good wife.'

As Anima wondered about tradition and the demands it placed on each person, Suhasini explained, 'Tradition connects us to our ancestors and the wisdom of the past. Without tradition, we are like a tree without roots. We dry up and die, knocked over by the slightest wind. Tradition is how we know who we are.'

Suhasini adjusted herself, tucking her feet underneath her body.

'But I know who I am.' Anima was sure. '*I am myself.*'

Suhasini smiled. 'Yes that's true, my love. But we are only what we are in relationship with the people around us, the places and the time we live in. God forbid if you lost your family, you would feel, act and *be* different.'

She paused briefly while Anima nodded. Then Suhasini continued, 'That is because we are all links in a long chain. Each link is necessary by itself, but only when linked with those around it does it become useful and strong. We are all connected and cannot be disconnected, even if you want to be. It is important right now, the world is changing, India is changing, even our traditions are changing.'

The British Raj stole so much from the people; not just food and spices and materials, but ideas. And ideas are the soul of the land. When ideas travel, they never return home the same. This became one of the greatest tragedies in the history of India.

As the traditions of India were exposed to the critique of the West, they were forced to adapt or die. The Western insistence on reason and science above all else sought to destroy elements of magic; the mystical elements of Mother India. This was the case with Vedanta.

In Indian spiritual tradition, Vedanta is the quest of the human soul to know the eternal and the infinite.[7] However, when the British arrived Vedanta came under pressure. In this situation, Ramakrishna Paramahamsa and Swami Vivekananda, especially, tried to uphold the ancient principles of Vedanta while adjusting as needed for a new and 'modern' frame.

Wisdom may be timeless and perfect, but it is taught to the afflicted human mind. Three important principles are given:

First is the belief that God realization is the ultimate goal of life; that we are here not for material gain or power or pleasure, but to know God. This God is the *self*—the true nature of the self, pure awareness, pure consciousness, *sat-chit-ananda*. The most important knowledge is *tat tvam asi*, that thou art—the famous expression of the relationship between the individual and the Absolute.

The second principle is that there is inherent divinity within the soul, which means that each of us is born with the ability to realize God. No one is more special than anyone else in God's eyes. Everyone is of the same essence.

And the third, that there is and can be harmony to the world's religions.

---

[7] Belur Math, 'Vedanta and Indian Culture', Belur Math, https://belurmath.org/vedanta-and-indian-culture/

There are four yogas as paths to gain knowledge of the true nature of the self.[8] Swami Vivekananda advocated this philosophy far and wide. Each person is different, so each path is different. Certain types of people may be drawn to one path over another, but the idea is that they all lead to the same place, which is seeing the divinity within ourselves.[9] These four yogas are the *karma yoga*, the path of action; *bhakti yoga*, the path of devotion; *raja yoga*, the path of meditation; and *jnana yoga*, the path of knowledge.

Alongside Vivekananda's synthesis of yogas was the teaching that morality is based on strength. He believed that weakness was the main cause of immoral behaviour, evil and suffering. This weakness could take many forms like violence, lying or greed, but the cause of all of it is ignorance about the true nature of the self. *This is why all the different paths lead to knowing the self.*

Little Anima would often tell her mother, 'I know who I am. I know myself.'

Suhasini would try to teach her daughter, 'Ah, but this is about knowing your *spiritual* self, not just your body and mind and what you like to eat.'

'How can I know that?'

'You follow the path of the four yogas. This is why they are so important. They lead us to our deepest spiritual self.'

'*Achchha*,' Anima said, though she did not really understand.

'The path to knowing our true self is not easy. It takes strength and determination. One of the best ways is by helping others instead of being selfish all the time.'

---

[8] Belur Math, 'Ideology', https://belurmath.org/ideology/
[9] Ibid.

Suhasini wanted her children to care for those around them. This focus on the welfare of others was emphasized by her beloved Ramakrishna Mission, whose aim was to serve all without any distinction of caste, religion, race or gender. This sense of care and consideration seeped into Anima's life and mind without her even knowing it. Equality and compassion were not always common in the past, or even now. Some still considered the equality of all people to be too progressive or unorthodox. Even in a high-caste family, it was rare to present daughters as worthy members of society. This hierarchy was a strongly rooted belief for many, and still flourishing widely.

The devaluing of daughters runs deep and strong throughout history. The birth of a daughter was a significant misfortune. The Atharva Veda offers a special mantra to help ensure the birth of a son rather than a daughter: 'The Lord of Creatures gives consent and active life to shape the embryo. May he place a male here and the birth of a girl elsewhere.'[10]

Many other ancient and sacred Hindu texts echo the calls for sons, saying daughters will bring nothing but harm to their fathers, and in the most extreme cases that they should be abandoned to the point of death.[11] Over the centuries, the idea of abandoning a daughter fell out of popularity and different interpretations arose to make sense of these sacred instructions. Rather than abandonment to death, it became important that a daughter was married properly. In this way, a

---

[10] Atharva Veda, 6.11.13. In 'Women In Hinduism'. Oxford Centre for Hindu Studies Online. Section 3. https://ochsonline.org/course/women-in-hinduism/

[11] 'Women in Hinduism', Oxford Centre for Hindu Studies Online. Section 3. https://ochsonline.org/course/women-in-hinduism/

daughter *abandoned* her birth family when she left to live with the family of her husband.

Suhasini was aware of the bold public proclamations of the time that were made about the need for women's social status to change. The last few decades had shown signs of change, but now, at the time her little Anima was growing up, progressive ideas had had some time to take root.

Back in the 1890s, Swami Vivekananda had addressed the dire conditions women were facing. 'There is no chance for the welfare of the world,' he insisted, 'unless the condition of women is improved. It is not possible for a bird to fly with only one wing.'[12] India needed both its men and women to meet their potential in order to soar. Swami Vivekananda went further, saying, 'Women must be put in a position to solve their own problems in their own way. No one can or ought to do this for them. And our Indian women are as capable of doing it as any in the world.'[13] This could only be brought about by education and an experience of the world outside the home. When asked if women had problems, Vivekananda responded saying that any problems women were facing could be 'solved by education'.[14]

'You must study, Anima,' Suhasini would say. 'You are alive at a time when so much is changing.'[15]

Suhasini strongly felt her daughter was lucky.

---

[12] Swami Vivekananda, *Teachings of Swami Vivekananda* (Kolkata: Advaita Ashrama, 2014), 125.

[13] Ibid., 135.

[14] Ibid., 129–30.

[15] There is no record of Reba's birth. It was common that records were not kept for girls. Some accounts have her born in 1930, others as late as 1940. Her school register stated she was born in 1934. Around this time is the most likely.

'But mostly I want to find the tallest tree and climb all the way up on my first try,' Anima replied with a mischievous smile. 'I want to run all the way home without stopping to catch my breath.'

'Sometimes, there is good fortune and luck in the world. You never know where you'll find it. You might feel it when you're climbing trees or running through the forest. Others might feel it somewhere else.'

'So, I am lucky?' Anima asked her mother.

'Yes you are, Reba.'

From then on, Anima was known as Reba.

Reba meaning lucky.

3

Calcutta—the New Home

A World Away from Comilla

In 1944, when Reba was still a child, she was sent away from Comilla to live with her uncle, Nagendra Chandra Rakshit, in Calcutta. A few years earlier, Jyotsna had made the trip. In those days, it was common for children to be sent by their family to live with a trusted guardian or family member in a bigger city. Sometimes it was necessary because of financial trouble or illness, which made it difficult for the householder to support an entire family. If there was a stable family member to live with, a move to a cultural or economic centre could open up new possibilities for the family. This was most common in larger families that had branches spread throughout the nation.

Reba and Jyotsna's parents thought that sending their daughters to the city would help secure a better future for them. Calcutta being the largest city in eastern India had the best to offer in education, business and the arts. The busy metropolis even had schools that accepted girls.

Reba and Jyotsna attended Peary Charan Girls' School in north Calcutta. Reba enrolled on 7 February 1944, shortly after arriving in Calcutta. The teachers called her by her given name, Anima. In the register, Nagendra Chandra Rakshit was listed as her guardian followed by her father's name. Five years prior, when Jyotsna had enrolled, she had listed one of the school's teachers as her guardian, with no family member present. The school was named after Peary Charan Sarkar, an alumni of the prestigious Hindu College in Calcutta. Apart from being a best-selling author, Sarkar was a member of Young Bengal, a free thought movement pioneered by the assistant headmaster of Hindu College Henry Louis Vivian Derozio. His ideas inspired a new generation of progressive intellectuals.[16] In an effort to uplift the condition of women, Sarkar founded the first free school for girls, Kalikrishna Girls' High School in 1847, just outside of Calcutta to the north-east.[17]

Reba's school was deep in the heart of north Calcutta, a stone's throw from the ancestral home of Swami Vivekananda, and close to the bustling book market in College Street and Calcutta University. Founded in 1868, the institution was pivotal for women's education in Bengal. It was established with only ten students and was originally named Chorbagan Balika Vidyalaya. It was renamed after the death of its founder in his honour.[18]

---

[16] David Kopf, *The Brahmo Samaj and the Shaping of the Modern Indian Mind* (Princeton, NJ: Princeton University Press, 1979), 42–43. See also, https://en.wikipedia.org/wiki/Peary_Charan_Sarkar

[17] Ravi N. Kadam, 'Empowerment of Women in India—An Attempt to Fill the Gender Gap', *International Journal of Scientific and Research Publications* 2, no. 6 (June 2012), 2.

[18] Peary Charan Girls' High School website. https://pearycharangirls.page4.me

The school stood tall and proud with bright blue pillars and a clear and bold sign marking the building. The land and building for Peary Charan Girls' School were donated by the sons of late Kalisadhan Pramanik. It is likely that this family was related to Tara Pramanik, a friend of Ishwar Chandra Vidyasagar. [19]

The school had a lovely, open courtyard. Each morning, Reba and Jyotsna separated here, each going their own way. Reba climbed the staircase and found her seat at a wooden desk, waiting for the teacher to start assigning the lessons.

The Rakshit sisters would walk to and from the school together daily. The distance between the school and their uncle's *bari* was short if they walked in a straight line but they rarely did that, choosing instead to wind their way through the alleyways of north Calcutta.

The girls would pass the various mess baris, or boarding houses, the small green Sarada Banerjee Park and schoolboys playing a game of cricket—they looked barely big enough to lift the bat, let alone swing it. They would also pass Simla Byayam Samity, a neighbourhood gymnasium, and often see students exercising. Eventually they would make their way back, settling in for the evening to study and rest. Sometimes, Calcutta felt like a world away from Comilla.

The Hooghly River was at the heart of Calcutta. A Calcuttan had the water of the Hooghly in their veins. The wideness of the river makes it a good path for ships coming upriver from the Bay of Bengal. So the Hooghly blesses

---

[19] 'Check Out These Centuries-old Kali Pujas of the City', *The Times of India*, October 2019, https://timesofindia.indiatimes.com/city/kolkata/check-out-these-centuries-old-kali-pujas-of-the-city/articleshow/71759118.cms

Calcutta twice: Once from the north, as the Ganga brings its life-giving water and spiritual purity from the distant Himalayas; and once from the south, as goods and people flow into and out of the city from anywhere in the world.

Downtown Calcutta dominated by the British Fort William near the riverbank and the expansive Maidan was lined with cafes selling milkshakes and sandwiches and the Oxford bookstore. But *uttor* Calcutta was the heart of the city. It spread beyond the newly constructed Howrah Bridge[20] to the canal,[21] and east to the Sealdah railway station, where the Rakshits and many others set foot in the city for the first time.

Nagendra Chandra Rakshit lived in the heart of north Calcutta—a hotbed of spiritual, social, artistic and political development. Its every street was lined with buildings three or four storeys high, their colourful facades streaked with dark mould from high humidity and long monsoon season. Countless tiny *dokan*s lined the walkways, selling coconuts, vegetables, sugar cane juice, etc. Be it sweetmeat shops, book shops, saree shops or shoe shops, all had their proprietors leaning on the doors and into the street, screaming, 'Come in! Good quality, cheap price!'

The streets of north Calcutta were filled with action and life. By mid-morning, men began gathering in small groups on the sidewalks, lighting coal fires under broad pans of oil for frying. They ate and talked, squatting or sitting on the pavement as the rest of the city walked by.

---

[20] Construction was completed in 1942.
[21] 'On The Drain Front … A Brief History of the City's Sewerage & Drainage System (1700s-1950s)', http://kolkatamunicipalcorporationblogs.blogspot.com/2015/04/on-drain-front-brief-history-of-citys_25.html

Trees grew right through the pavements, crumbling the concrete and leaving big holes in the path. The city smelled of a million people with their cooking fires, spices, incense and automobiles. The odours of coal smoke and car exhaust were inescapable. The traffic would be dense and chaotic. At first, Reba was afraid to try to cross a busy street as cars, people, bikes, cows, rickshaws, dogs and goats all swerved around one another trying to carve out their own path.

She quickly learned where the river was and how the main streets ran parallel to it, so she could always measure where she was in this hectic new place according to how many blocks away she was from the ghats that led to the water. The fishy smell of the river and the coolness of the air increased as she got closer to the Hooghly. She longed to dive in, practise her swimming strokes and float on her back, but the river ghat was often busy in the mornings. And she had her school to attend. Although Reba fervently worked to orient herself in the city, sometimes she was left deeply longing for the forest outside Comilla. Back home, she measured the days by the sun rising in the east and setting in the west. But the tall, closely packed buildings in Calcutta made the sunrise much harder to see and Goddess Usha's warmth harder to appreciate.

At that time, lakhs of young men were flocking to the city, looking for jobs, education or inspiration. If they were not as lucky as Reba and Jyotsna, and did not have a family member to stay with, they often lived in mess baris that were scattered throughout north Calcutta.[22] The mess baris sprang to life all

---

[22] Mess is English refers to the room where soldiers eat and bari means house in Bangla. Mouni Mondal, 'Walking into Kolkata's Iconic Mess-Baris', 7 March 2022, https://www.getbengal.com/details/walking-into-iconic-mess-baris-of-kolkata-city. See also, Bitan Sikdar, 'Inside the Messbaris That Inspired Byomkesh Bakshi's

over the city in the late nineteenth and early twentieth centuries. The name mess bari, a combination of English and Bengali words, is one of the countless signs of how intertwined the two cultures were. In these places, people from various backgrounds, who could not afford to have their own home, gathered and lived together under one roof for months or even years. For a nominal monthly fee, men could live, be fed and have basic amenities provided for them. They stayed in the vibrant city during the week and returned to their *desher* bari, their rural family home, on the weekends. The mess baris were located near the busy areas of north Calcutta, like Amherst Street, College Street, Maniktala and Sealdah, where the tenants could stay close to their workplace. They came to Calcutta from the suburbs to work as clerks, salesmen, lawyers or professors. Some were poets, writers or artists. Even political activists took refuge in the mess baris to avoid arrest by the authorities. Some came without specific employment, hoping that once they were established in Calcutta they could look for work or attend school.

Nagendra *kaka*'s bari was right off of one of the first big streets from the river, Harrison Road, at Peary Mohan Pal Lane.[23] Near his bari was also Vivekananda Road, a busy street that cut across north Calcutta all the way to the river, where it finally stopped near the Jagannath Ghat and the proud new bridge—Howrah Bridge. Every time she saw the name of Vivekananda Road, Reba thought of her mother sitting with

---

Quarters', 13 October 2018, https://www.telegraphindia.com/culture/inside-the-messbaris-that-inspired-byomkesh-bakshi-s-quarters/cid/1671771. See also, 'Go see a Kolkata "Mess Bari" before it Vanishes', 31 August, 2021, https://www.getbengal.com/details/go-see-a-kolkata-mess-bari-before-it-vanishes

[23] Harrison Road became Mahatma Gandhi road later.

her legs tucked underneath her, telling stories about the great man. Swami Vivekananda's ancestral home was less than a kilometre from her uncle's house. *Ma would love to see this*! Reba thought with a pang of sadness. She liked walking by the house and reciting the four yogas to herself: 'Karma, Raja, Bhakti, Jnana. Karma, Raja, Bhakti, Jnana.'

And at this moment, she felt that she was in the centre of the universe, as though standing completely still while the rest of the world spun around her.

Swami Vivekananda and his teacher Ramakrishna Paramahamsa were responsible for so much in her life, and in the life of Calcutta, her new home. The city felt so alive. With each day in this new place, she could feel the passing of time.

The constant push for Indian independence made the Age of Darkness, the Kali Yoga, palpable all over the city. This crowded city, named after the powerful and destructive Goddess Kali, was also home of great sages who transcended time and culture.

Goddess Kali's presence permeates the city of Calcutta. Some believe that the Bengali version of the name Calcutta—Kalikata—is derived from *Kalikshetra* meaning 'Ground of the Goddess Kali'.[24]

To Reba, the city felt not only loud, dirty and crowded, but also exciting and full of opportunites.

Some days Calcutta could feel like an island of peace, while on other days it could feel chaotic. It was home to many religions and a vast array of cultural traditions. Prior to the arrival of the British in the eighteenth century and

---

[24] Britannica, 'Kolkata', Britannica, https://www.britannica.com/place/Kolkata

Christianity along with it, the Bengal region was under the control of Muslim sultans. So along with many forms of Hinduism, Islam had thrived. Reaching back in time even further, Hindu and Buddhist rulers had governed the region. All those cultures and religions lived side by side, making for a diverse and sometimes overwhelming mix.[25]

---

[25] Glen Alexander Hayes, 'Eroticism and Cosmic Transformation as Yoga: The *Atmatattva* of the Vaisnava Sahajiyas of Bengal', in *Yoga in Practice*, ed. David Gordon White (Princeton, NJ: Princeton University Press, 2012), 224.

4

Bengal in the Aftermath of Hindu Renaissance

An Era of Viewing Traditions through the Lens of *Reason And Logic*

The presence of the goddesses Durga and Kali was everywhere in Calcutta. Massive pandals were built every Fall to honour Durga Ma. Rural artisans spent months making the statues for Durga Puja, using bamboo, cloth, clay or any other material deemed sturdy. The pandals were then adorned with any number of things including papier mâché, paint, fabric or recycled materials in bright and celebratory colours. During Durga Puja, the city would shut down to celebrate the goddess. But Kali's presence was more steady, both in Kalighat, the heart of Calcutta, and north of the city in Dakshineswar.

Many families chose to visit Dakshineswar temple at the most auspicious time, Kali Puja, the festival celebrating the goddess.

The temple was quite far away from the city. Just as the sun was setting, families would make their way, by whatever means they could, north towards the temple.

The traffic slowed to a crawl near the temple as the road was packed with taxis, rickshaws and people moving in the same direction—the temple.

Near the entrance to the courtyard, drums and singing filled the air, the mood ecstatic in devotion. Inside the walls, the drumming and singing were loudest. There was a small bright white shrine that seemed to glow as the crowd crossed the courtyard. It was dedicated to Rani Rashmoni, the founder of the Dakshineswar Kali Temple.

Rani Rashmoni, born in 1793, came from a poor, low-caste family in a village near Calcutta called Kuna. At the age of eleven, she married a rich zamindar from Calcutta. Rashmoni's husband was a follower of the liberal and reformist ideals of Ram Mohan Roy, who founded the Brahmo Samaj. He shared his intellectual endeavours with his wife and consequently Rashmoni became well-versed in the cultural and social issues of the time. Then her husband died and Rashmoni inherited his massive estate. She was about to make the pilgrimage to Varanasi when she had a dream, complete with a vision of what to do next. Rashmoni's vision was that she needed to construct a temple for Goddess Kali.

Rashmoni was in good standing with the community, seen as a generous and courageous patron, but she was a woman of low caste by birth. Despite having paid for and organized its construction, the temple had to be dedicated to a Brahmin in order to have the idol installed. So the temple was dedicated to her guru, Ramkumar, a Brahmin priest and the elder brother of Ramakrishna. However, Ramkumar passed away in the following year, leaving the temple in charge of Ramakrishna who initially accepted it with great reluctance.

Ramakrishna did not represent himself as a holy man normally would. He neither draped himself in saffron nor did he wear polished slippers. He slept on a simple bed covered by a mosquito netting.[26] He spent vast amounts of time in spiritual pursuits.

Ramakrishna was in Dakshineswar for several decades before his cult of followers grew. He led the temple, serving as an ardent devotee of Goddess Kali and a leader in the religious culture of Bengal. Ramakrishna attracted many middle-class, educated Hindus who were drawn to learn from the living saint. One curious young man, Narendranath, became a disciple after falling into a powerful trance with Ramakrishna's feet placed on his chest.[27] He was a member of the Brahmo Samaj movement and who would soon become known to the world as Swami Vivekananda.

Reba was born near the end of the Hindu Renaissance, when Indians were working to prove what was *true* through the lens of reason and logic, even in regard to the Vedas. It was a time when social customs were changing and coming under question among different visions of morality.

The fathers of modern India like Raja Ram Mohan Roy tried to bring tradition into harmony with modernity.[28] Vedanta was considered to be the culmination of the wisdom of the Vedas and therefore one of India's greatest treasures. They wanted to show that Vedanta and Hinduism were as great as

---

[26] Sumit Sarkar, 'Ramakrishna and the Calcutta of his Times', *India International Centre Quarterly* 17, nos 3, 4 (Winter 1990/91), 100.

[27] Gavin Flood, *An Introduction to Hinduism* (Cambridge, UK: Cambridge University Press, 1996), 257.

[28] Ibid., 250–51.

Christianity or Islam, or even better; that these traditions were ethical and powerful.

A 'new' Hinduism argued that all religions believe in a transcendent God, and the differences between religions are small. Ultimately, everything is *brahman*, complete oneness. At the root of all belief, God is one. However, in British India, the belief had to be infused with reason.

Ramakrishna also believed that all religions were essentially one. So, the worship of Goddess Kali was the worship of brahman. The Brahmo Samaj also endorsed this view. Ramakrishna preached this message, 'As one and the same material, water, is called by different names ... So, the one *sat-chit-ananda*, the everlasting-intelligent-bliss, is invoked by some as God, by some as Allah, by some as Hari and by others Brahman.'[29]

Swami Vivekananda too believed that oneness permeates everything, all existence. He taught that we should love everything and everyone because all beings are innately divine. He presented this doctrine to the World Parliament of Religions in Chicago in 1893; it is the cornerstone of the Vedanta Society of New York, which he founded in 1895 followed by the Ramakrishna Mission in India two years later.[30]

In 1828, Roy founded the Brahmo Samaj in an effort to 'restore' Hinduism to its rightful ways of reason and ethics. It opposed idol worship, sati and child marriage. Practices were reformed which largely concerned what women could and could not do, including child marriage and sati. Many who lived in the villages or who were illiterate held tightly to their

---

[29] Max Müller, *Ramakrishna: His Life and Sayings* (Kolkata: Advaita Ashrama, 2014), 98.
[30] Flood, *An Introduction to Hinduism*, 258.

devotional practices. Thus, he did not connect deeply with rural people or the poor, despite his appeal to Brahmins.[31]

After Roy's death, Rabindranath Tagore's father Debendranath Tagore and Keshab Chandra Sen continued the reform movement. Tagore agreed with the move away from rituals and the worship of deities, embracing the absolute and unknowable oneness as the rightful focus of spirituality. Sen suggested equality between high and low caste, but this was a problem for many who felt it was a step too far.

This new form of Hinduism, or Neo-Vedanta, became popular among the middle class, especially the English-speaking. And this new Hinduism was closely tied to yoga. Many definitions and practices of yoga went back centuries, into the sacred Upanishads, the Bhagavadgita and even into the philosophies of Buddhism and Jainism. Hence, it was easy for Swami Vivekananda to formulate and teach his four paths of yoga.

Yoga was taught by Swami Vivekananda as the ultimate goal of all mankind. He said that the aim and end of all religions is union with God. While the aim is one, the method of attaining it may vary with the different temperaments of men.[32] Both the goal and the methods employed for reaching it are called yoga. Yoga was the method of union.

Swami Vivekananda stressed that though the four paths of yogas may be different, they end up in the same place. The branches of yoga, like tributaries of a river, flow into the same ocean. Even though they start in different places and flow in seemingly different directions, they all end in the same place and become one. They are all made of the same water.

---

[31] Ibid., 254.
[32] Vivekananda, *Teachings of Swami Vivekananda*, 293.

Post-Independence India—A Nation on the Churn

5

Reba Joins the Movement of Body, Spirit And Country

An Attempt to Build Indian Identity through Bodily Purity

As Reba grew through her teenage years and into adulthood, Calcutta became consumed with building strong and healthy bodies. Even a spiritual leader like Swami Vivekananda insisted that India's problems began with physical weakness and illness.[33] 'There is no way to be intelligent or productive,' he said, 'unless you are strong first. First build up your physique, only then can you get control over the mind.' He even suggested that the physically weak were unfit for spiritual practice and the realization of the spiritual self. So Calcutta, and the rest of India, intently pursued physical culture to make their bodies strong.

---

[33] Swami Vivekananda, *Complete Works of Swami Vivekananda* (Kolkata: Advaita Ashrama, 2002), 155.

Across akharas, a healthy mind in a healthy body echoed in the air as young men lunged and squatted, paraphrasing the old Latin.[34]

The body is the instrument for all good deeds[35] rang through their minds as they lifted weights, quoting the Indian poet Kalidasa. These clubs that promoted physical health through *byayam* and other physical cultures, sprang to life as vital cultural centres.

The obsession with health and strength was largely a reaction to the British who had portrayed Indian men as weak and degenerate. This portrayal was spearheaded by an Englishman named Herbert Risley, a member of the Indian Civil Service. He analysed and categorized the size and character of the Bengalis' biological features, made classifications of the population's race, caste and tribe, and then used the findings to construct a hierarchical race structure.[36] Following Risley, journalists insulted the robustness of the Bengali physique and even their value as humans. One journalist wrote, 'The Bengali's leg is either skin and bone, the same size all the way down, with knocking knobs for knees, or else is very fat and globular, also turning in at the knees, with round thighs like a woman's. The Bengali's leg is the leg of a slave. Except by grace of his natural masters, a slave he always has been and always must be.'[37] A common British jab was that Bengalis were a lowly people from a low-lying land.[38]

---

[34] The Latin is *mens sana in corpore sano*.

[35] The Sanskrit transliteration is *shariramadyam khalu dharmasadhanam* from Kalidasa's *Kumarasambhavam*.

[36] Sir Herbert Risley — Royal Anthropological Institute. https://www.therai.org.uk/archives-and-manuscripts/obituaries/herbert-risley

[37] G.W. Steevens, *In India* (London: William Blackwood and Sons, 1900), 75–76.

[38] John Roselli, 'The Self-Image of Effeteness: Physical Education

The attempts to make the Bengalis think that they were inherently weak or inferior to their colonizers were brutal beyond measure. These cut deep into the hearts of the Bengalis. Many saw these insults as vicious misrepresentation and set out to prove the stereotype wrong. Thus, the physical culture movement intertwined with a call to nationalism and to strengthen the Indian identity.

In 1866, Rajnarayan Basu began the process by reviving the practice of national gymnastics exercises, making physical culture a central goal of the Nationality Promotion Society. Basu wanted to prove that the Bengalis had organizational intelligence and military prowess. Shortly after, the influential Tagore family launched a festival in Calcutta in conjunction with the Hindu Mela that centred on sporting events, valuable for instilling health and activity in Indian youth.[39] From the start, Nabagopal Mitra, the chief organizer of the mela, promoted gymnastics, wrestling and other traditional sports. Over the years, he trained a number of physical education teachers and founded several akharas. The festival attracted a lot of attention including that of Motilal Ghosh, the co-founder of *Amrita Bazar Patrika*. Unfortunately, this festival died out around the 1870s, but that did not slow the momentum of the physical culture movement. New gyms, clubs and societies kept popping up to support the growing trend. The movement even grew to include women.

Sarala Debi, the niece of Rabindranath Tagore, who had participated actively in the Hindu Mela, took to the cause of

---

and Nationalism in Nineteenth-Century Bengal', *Past & Present* 86 (February 1980), 121–48.

[39] Ibid., 127, 129.

education, physical and otherwise, for both men and women.[40] She worked to create an all-India women's organization which would be formed and run by women. She focused intently on the question of 'woman power'. Displays of strength, like any woman who could lift heavy weights or objects, were powerful tools to capture an audience's attention and therefore to influence the popular perception. In this way, community members who exemplified strength were increasingly important to the cause. Sarala Debi wrote that women's power is a source of enormous strength in any country, and no nation can progress by ignoring it. If the energy of women is allowed to be dormant, how can a nation be inspired to achieve its potential? Therefore, *to stir and stimulate women into action is a priority*, she wrote.[41] She praised the goddess, assuring women that they were embodiments of such power and authority.

Sarala Debi intertwined the feminist cause with Indian nationalism, philosophy and religion. She was political and drew inspiration from nationalist military leaders. She inherited the remnants of the Sakhi Samiti, a branch of the Ladies' Theosophical Society, which was established by her mother Swarnakumari Debi.[42] Sarala Debi often incorporated physical culture displays into festivals like Durga Puja. She also shared Swami Vivekananda's belief that physical strength was the means to a strong nation.[43]

---

[40] Ronojoy Sen, 'Breaking the Stereotype', *Outlook India*, 4 February 2022, https://www.outlookindia.com/website/story/breaking-the-stereotype/296142

[41] Bharati Ray, *Early Feminists of Colonial India* (New Delhi: Oxford University Press, 2012), 79.

[42] Ibid., 78.

[43] Roselli, 'The Self-Image of Effeteness, 130.

This way, Sarala Debi inspired the next generation of nationalist leaders at the turn of the twentieth century. The Anusilan Samiti (a bodybuilding society) was founded in 1902, and was built around a more extreme idea of nationalism that sometimes veered into outright violence and terrorism.[44] Part of its conception of the Indian identity was bodily purity, a traditional belief often linked to religion and spirituality. The organization grew out of youth groups and developed into a society that promoted self-discipline, bodybuilding and *lathi khela* (stick training), and was often paired with vows of austerity and celibacy. Like so many others at the time, the Anusilan Samiti held the belief that strength of character was determined by health of the body. True intelligence was impossible without health.[45] This link between bodily strength, spiritual purity and nationalism was key to the promotion of yoga.

In the early part of the twentieth century, yoga was not yet a popular practice as it was more closely linked with religion, spiritual development and ultimately liberation from the cycle of suffering, or *samsara*. However, as the decades of the twentieth century advanced, physical practices were gaining popularity. Parallel to the Hindu reform movements and the Bengali renaissance, yoga became a perfect vehicle for the transformation.

Just as Vivekananda was influenced by both the progressive Brahmo Samaj and the mystic Ramakrishna, yoga became a tool for liberation in two different, sometimes

---

[44] Keka Dutta Roy, 'From Terrorism to Socialism: The Role of the Anushilan Samiti (1935–47)', *Proceedings of the Indian History Congress*, Vol. 69 (2008), 574–86.

[45] Roselli, The Self-Image of Effeteness, 131.

opposing, senses of the word. In the historic sense of spiritual transcendence, yoga reflected its traditional use of gaining freedom from the constraints of the material world. But a new and practical form of independence was becoming more urgent for Bharat Mata, that of Indian national independence from colonial rule. Teachers of yoga like Swami Vivekananda drew upon traditions and added new meaning along the way. Any attempt at freedom was yoga. This combination of body, spirit and country was central to the belief of Pulin Behari Das who ran the Dacca (now Dhaka) branch of the Anusilan Samiti. It was Pulin Behari Das who gave Nilmoni Das, a north Calcutta pioneer of physical culture, his historic title 'Iron Man'. The title had nationalist significance but was also fitting because Das lived in the 'Iron District' of north Calcutta, near Peary Charan Girls' School, Vivekananda's ancestral home and Ghosh's College of Physical Education.

Before rising as a leader of physical culture, bodybuilding and yoga in Calcutta, Das trained in clubs and gyms as a young man. He often gave public demonstrations of barbell exercises at neighbourhood festivals and pujas. His work caught the attention of Jaladhar Sen, the editor of *Monthly India* magazine, who thought that Das's work was important and groundbreaking. He encouraged Das to publish something about physical training so that others could learn, thereby influencing a wider range of Indians. He said that Das should include photographs of the exercises along with written instruction, which would make the publication more attractive and easier to use. But photography was very expensive at the time, and Das was not wealthy. However, his aunt agreed to sell off her jewellery to pay for the photos. Das's first publication was a wall chart of barbell exercises.

Three thousand copies of its initial print run were quaterly sold.[46] From that day onwards, Das was a staple of north Calcutta and the surrounding regions, popular as an expert in physical education. He even started his own school and published many books on exercise and yoga.

In the 1930s, while Reba Rakshit was a child, Das wrote one of the first guides of physical culture for women. The *Amrita Bazar Patrika* printed his *Physical Training for Women*, which contained photos of his wife Reba Das dressed in a saree, flexing her biceps, demonstrating poses and bending an iron rod.[47] 'A nation's health depended on the sum total of male and female,' he wrote. India could not be a strong country if the women were not taught physical culture side by side with the men. He vigorously advocated sound mind and sound body. He wrote, 'Weak women will produce weak children and no country has ever developed into greatness without bi-sexual [*sic*] physical fitness, with both the men and women healthy and strong.'[48]

The inclusion of women into the nationalist cause was another reason for the modern rise of yoga.[49] More and more leaders of the Indian Independence movement emphasized that the battle required unity. If half of the society—the women—were weak or excluded from the efforts, the thrust for independence was also weakened by half. 'Yoga is a method of union,' Vivekananda had said. He was referring to the union

---

[46] Swapan Das (Nilmoni Das's son) in an interview with the author, 21 July 2020.
[47] *Amrita Bazar Patrika*. Vol. 68, No 127 (17 May 1936), British Library, EAP262/1/1/34/17, https://eap.bl.uk/archive-file/EAP262-1-1-34-17
[48] Ibid.
[49] Ida Jo Pajunen, 'Yoga in Bengal', *Journal of Yoga Studies* (forthcoming).

of the individual with God, but it was easily extrapolated to serve the double meaning of a unified India, men and women.

Just across the street from Peary Charan Girls' School and near the school of Nilmoni Das was another important centre Simla Byayam Samity.

The Simla Byayam Samity was founded in 1926 by Atindra Nath Bosu with the goal to build healthy and morally courageous Bengali youths. The objective was both nationalist and humanitarian—the sons and daughters of India could fight for the freedom movement of the motherland at any time and they could give help to those who were weak or needed aid.[50]

The Simla Byayam Samity originally taught bodybuilding mainly, but later wrestling, *lathi khela* and other sports were introduced. It also incorporated religious elements into the training, combining the physical with the spiritual. Bosu introduced the Sarbojanin Durgotsav which not only encouraged the youths to worship Ma Durga, but also taught that Ma Durga belonged to everyone, not just the rich or the zamindars or the high caste. Since his goals were more egalitarian, the Simla Byayam Samity organized events so that everyone, regardless of their social standing, had the chance to participate in the freedom struggle against the British government. Bosu worked closely with other revolutionary leaders like Aurobindo Ghose, and was imprisoned several times for his actions in the independence movement.

There was a lot of support and praise for the Simla Byayam Samiti in Calcutta especially in the north. The *Calcutta Municipal Gazette* wrote in 1929: 'Calcutta must be covered

---

[50] Simla Byayam Samity, History & Tradition, http://simlabyayamsamity.com/history.html#history

by gymnasiums like Simla Byayam Samity before we can hope to see our young men stand with their heads erect and walk with their chests forward.'[51] But it was not just the young men, female members of the club were equally skilled in fighting with sticks. And a few of them were even freedom fighters.

Around the time of Reba's arrival in Calcutta, Jatiya Krira O Sakti Sangha became active in her uncle's neighbourhood. It had the following aim: 'To build up future citizens of a free India full of nationalism, patriotism and idealism.'[52] The founder Shambhu Nath Mallick's objective was development of the youth through sport and education. Reba eagerly took part in the activities and camps organized by the the sangha. There were sports, adult education and training in *bratachari*.

The Bratachari Movement was another product of the nationalist momentum of the era.[53] Founded in 1932 by Gurusaday Dutt, it aimed to raise the self-esteem and national awareness of people regardless of their religion, caste, gender or age. It was a comprehensive programme of physical, mental and intellectual culture based on folk traditions of physical exercise, art, dance, drama, music, singing and social service. *Brata* means a sacred vow and *chari* means the person who is dedicated to it. This strong emphasis on the equality in religion, caste and especially gender contributed greatly in reshaping modern India.

Reba was also actively involved in parades, celebrations and rifle shooting. And it was in these spheres that Reba's unique talent was first spotted by others.[54]

---

[51] Ibid.
[52] http://www.khamarparajatiyakriraosaktisangha.com/school.php
[53] See https://en.wikipedia.org/wiki/Bratachari_movement.
[54] Rakshit, 'The Sport of Elephant Lifting', 253–264.

Reba registered for a shooting competition organized by the Kasimbazar Rifle Club. She arrived for the competition with a .22 rifle and an unwavering sense of accuracy and determination, and left with a gold medal—a rare feat of the era.[55]

In the early years of the 1960s, Godai Chand Mullick, a champion rifle shooter closely associated with the Bengal Rifle Association, decided within a short notice that his wife Geeta Mullick will participate in the upcoming National Rifle Competition. She was a stout, fair-skinned woman often seen with a bright sindoor in the middle parting of her hair. She was barely able to hold the rifle, and certainly never considered shooting a weapon among her goals in life.[56]

Godai told her of his idea, she was stunned.

'What would people say, what would they think! I am a housewife!'

She was immensely worried about people mocking her.

'Don't worry, I will be by your side,' he replied. 'Twenty days is more than enough to make you an expert!'

They began intense preparations.

When the D-Day arrived, Geeta understandably had butterflies in her stomach. Godai reassured her, 'Do not worry, winning and losing are both part of the game.'

He stood firmly behind her encouraging her through every move.

She fired the rifle.

Followed by a brief pause.

Then she fired a second time.

---

[55] Ibid.
[56] 'A New Name on the List of Bengali Female Brave-Hearts', *Byayam Charcha*, Year 1, Issue 6. Bengali year 1371. Gregorian year 1964–65.

In both the slow and rapid firing competition, she surpassed every other competitor.

Then came the general group competition, far more challenging than the first round. Again, Geeta beat nearly all the competitors—including her husband—and was placed second in the competition.

Godai laughed, 'Only a guru knows the joys of such a defeat!'

Thus, Geeta's name was added to the Bengali female bravehearts who were increasingly pushing the boundaries even further.

'Geeta, what about the Olympics? Will you go to Tokyo in '64?'

Already, the crowds were getting ahead of themselves.

'It will be my husband who decides. Now I am quite happy and have my two daughters and son to look after,' she had replied.

'Godai Babu, will she go to the Olympics?' they asked her husband.

He explained that she would not go.

'India lags behind in pistol shooting and is looked down upon on the world's stage. We have to work hard to achieve the international standards, otherwise we shall make a fool of ourselves in front of the world! So for now, going for the Olympics is a distant dream.'

Geeta chimed in. 'Do we have the necessary weapons? The expert teachers? Trainers?'

There was precision in her words.

'Besides, the cost of bullets is sky-high! Imagine every time we shoot a bullet we worry how much money we have lost. How poor have we become!'

Her victory speech had turned serious. Striking at the heart of so many issues, she pressed on.

'Moreover, I have not seen much appreciation and encouragement for ladies to pick up this sport.'

She paused as the words rang out.

'It has always been men shooters who have been invited by the Indian government. No female shooter has ever come to this land, whether from Russia, Sweden or any other Western country. So one has to conclude that the Indian government is not keen on women taking up shooting as a sport and does not wish to encourage such thoughts in the mind of the public!'

This started to gnaw at some of those who were gathering.

'Oh, this is your hurt pride speaking!'

One man cried out, blaming her bitterness on the gold she had missed out.

'Give it any name you wish, but you cannot wish away the truth.'

With that final word, Geeta retreated. She had been away from home for quite some time and household chores awaited her even as the clock ticked towards midnight.

Another asked her as she walked to the door, 'Will you keep up your practice?'

Geeta answered, 'I would love to. But looking after a whole family takes up most of the time. Children, their studies, cooking … these are my first priorities.'

The community of physical culturists was close-knit. All of the clubs and centres in north Calcutta were close to one another, and their leaders were well known in the area, as were the star students and athletes. Local performances were common.

Those who lived in the community watched the parades, worshipped at the community pujas and were awed by the displays of strength, discipline and skill.

Around this time, there was another organization developing in north Calcutta that would soon become the centre of Reba's life. Founded in 1923, this institution had a knack for putting on performances that captured the audience's wide-eyed attention. Its founder, Bishnu Charan Ghosh, was a charismatic and talented coach who was known for spotting and nurturing talent. It was Ghosh who had inspired Nilmoni Das to take up yoga in addition to weightlifting and bodybuilding. It was Ghosh who wrote for *Byayam Charcha,* a popular health magazine published by Shambhu Mallick, founder of Jatiyo Krira O Sakti Sangha. Ghosh had his finger on the pulse of the region; he knew how to draw large crowds and create striking displays of skill that inspired the curiosity in people. He knew bodybuilding and muscle control were popular, and he was on the cutting edge of fitness trends as well.

Ghosh could change a person's destiny. Many of his young pupils came from a life that was supposedly doomed, predestined to failure. Yet, he pulled so many such souls out of their drowning lives. If it were not for him, they might have spent their days hungry, wondering where they would get their next meal. While his brother Swami Paramahansa Yogananda was away injecting Eastern spirituality into Western lands, Ghosh was primarily on his home soil, training and developing the sons and daughters of the land.

Ghosh deeply cared for his students—saving the milk from his domesticated cow for the young boys who had finished their weightlifting sessions. He was hit hard when he lost his young son and father in the same year. He had a tenderness about him, underneath all his rippling muscles. His care may sometimes appear harsh despite being directed towards his students in all sincerity. Either way, he changed the course of lives for those who were lucky.

Reba was one of them.

Reba was just nearing her teenage years when she arrived at Ghosh's College of Physical Education, and from that moment her life would never be the same.

6

Finding Her Guru—Bishnu Charan Ghosh

A Journey from Darkness to Light

On the day Reba visited Ghosh's college a special puja was being organized. Much of the neighbourhood was gathered nearby, crowding the dead-end alley and pushing towards the gate and the towering archway. The sign above the gate could be seen from the end of the alley. In big block letters, it read: Ghosh's College of Physical Education.

As Reba approached the gate, she could hear the slamming of weights against the ground, which sounded like a car falling out of the sky or a building collapsing. *A person can lift something that heavy*! Reba thought. There were shrieks of encouragement from the onlookers. She pressed her way inside the gate, towards the front of the crowd.

The ground floor gym opened onto a small courtyard. The space was full of muscular men and various metal bars loaded with weights. In the middle was a single bar that seemed to be the heaviest. Its ends were loaded with several thick weighted discs. This was clearly the centre of attention at the moment; every face in the crowd looked towards the bar with eager anticipation. After a moment, one of the muscular men walked slowly from the edge of the courtyard towards the bar. He stopped behind it, the bar touching his shins. He lifted one arm and waved to the crowd, smiling.

All around her, voices were shouting with reverence and awe for what they were witnessing. *That man must be famous*, she thought.

The man took several fast breaths, pumping his chest up and down and puffing his cheeks. His face had a look of intensity, his eyes were blind to everything around him, staring blankly forward. He bent down. He wrapped his fingers around the bar carefully, one at a time starting with each index finger. He took one last breath and then exploded with energy as he pulled the bar upwards. He drew the bar off the ground in one powerful motion as he straightened his legs and stood up. But he did not stop there. He grunted loudly and lifted it quickly to his shoulders with a little hop. The weighted discs rattled as the bar landed on his chest; the bar bent slightly under the weight.

The crowd erupted, cheering, yelling and shouting. Reba was caught up in the emotion of the crowd and the surprise at the man's strength. She cheered!

But the man was not done yet. He took a couple of more fast breaths, holding the bar on his chest, clearly straining under the weight, his face reddening more with each second. Then he gritted his teeth, bent his knees slightly and exploded upwards again. It was like he was trying to throw the weight straight upwards into the sky. He straightened his legs and pushed the bar up with his arms. As the bar was moving, he bent down again, ducking underneath it. He split his legs apart from front to back; his left leg going backwards and his right coming forwards. At the same time he straightened his arms and caught the bar overhead. He wobbled a bit, trying to catch his balance and control of the heavy weight. His arms stabilized, and finally he stepped his feet together and straightened his legs triumphantly. He stood straight up with the bar all the way over his head. The crowd broke into yells of surprise and delight. The muscular man gave a huge grin and looked around briefly before stepping back and letting the weight fall to the ground in front of him. It crashed down to the earth with a tremendous rattling thud.

Reba could feel the earth shake. The barbell bounced a couple of times before finally coming to rest in the middle of the courtyard. The man raised his arms overhead and grinned as the crowd cheered its adulation.

Reba was intoxicated with admiration. This man was both powerful and revered. *This must be a very good gym*, she thought.

As the crowd calmed down, Reba squeezed through to the front and saw a man who seemed to work there. She heard him saying, 'Everyone will need to speak to the principal, Byayamacharya Ghosh. He can turn any talented student into a star.'

Then he pointed to some equipment on the ground. 'Look! These are the first of their kind. Sandow dumb-bells.'

They were little bars that could be held in one hand, with round weights on each end. The bar itself was split in two lengthwise and spring loaded, so when you picked it up you would have to squeeze it together with your hand, challenging the grip. The man explained that the weights were new, developed by the German bodybuilder Sandow. 'Some people think they're worthless and that they will never catch on.'

Just as Reba was wondering where to go next, the man announced, 'Weightlifting and bodybuilding are here on the ground floor,' he said, 'yoga is upstairs.'

Reba was overwhelmed with the big building and the excitement all around.

'The way to the first floor is from there.'

He pointed to the left side of the courtyard where a steep and narrow staircase climbed up the side of the building.

'The yoga practice rooms are there. You can ask at the top of the stairs. The men's room is to the right and the women's room is to the left, down the narrow hall. Also, there is the office where Byayamacharya Ghosh works.'

Just as he was about to walk away, the air filled with a long and loud *mooooooooooooooo*. Next to the gym was a big cow that Reba had not noticed until now. She was startled.

The man laughed and said, 'Oh, don't let her surprise you. We keep her close by because we need her milk. It helps make our muscles big and strong.'

Reba carefully walked around the edge of the courtyard until she reached the stairs. When she entered the school's first floor, she walked through the outer door and up another short flight of stairs to the lobby area where there was a small table with a young woman sitting behind it. To the left, Reba could hear several women counting. She looked but only saw a long hallway.

'1 … 2 … 3… 4… 5 … 6 … 7 … 8 … 9 … 10. 1 … 2 … 3 …'

The women's voices counted to ten over and over again in a sharp, clear manner. To her right was a very short hallway, and a few men's voices speaking and counting.

'Namaskar,' Reba said to a young woman. 'I would like to learn. *Ektu amake ki shekhaben* (Can you teach me too?) ?'

'Very good, ma'am,' the young woman replied. 'First you will meet with the principal to determine your exercises. The women practise down the hallway to your left.'

She lifted her right arm, pointed down the hall and said, 'You are welcome to go look into the women's room, ma'am.'

'Achchha,' Reba said.

She turned and walked slowly down the hallway. At the end, a door opened into a large room. In the room, there was a row of women sitting in chairs, counting and watching the others who were doing various exercises. *They must be the teachers*, thought Reba.

'One! To the right,' said the teacher closest to the door. An older woman in front of her twisted her body to the right.

'Two! In the middle.'

The student untwisted her body and returned to the middle.

'Three! To the left.'

She twisted to the left.

'Four! In the middle …'

There were two other women in the room doing different exercises. A younger girl was standing, kicking her legs forward one at a time. First the right, then the left. A middle-aged woman was seated on the floor behind the others, on a thin-cushioned mattress. She was stretching both her legs straight forward like sticks; she reached forward with her hands, touching her toes.

One of the teachers sitting at the front of the room looked at Reba and nodded her head without stopping her count: 'Six … seven … eight …' Reba nodded and then returned down the hallway to the lobby. As she reached the central room, a short, well-dressed man exited the office and took a few steps towards her. He had broad shoulders and finely groomed hair that was combed straight back off his forehead. His round face looked familiar to her, but she could not quite place it.

Suddenly, she realized this was the same man whose picture was on the wall. He was the founder and the principal of the school, a celebrity of north Calcutta. This was Bishnu Charan Ghosh.

'Do you want to learn yoga?'

He got right to the point.

Reba was taken aback by his directness.

'Yes, sir. I want to learn. But I don't know anything about it.'

He did not seem troubled by her response at all. He said confidently, 'Don't worry, I will teach you.'[57]

A couple weeks later, Reba arrived home from school to meet her grandfather standing at the front door squinting in the late afternoon light.

'Come, Reba. Tonight is your first lesson. I will take you to Ghosh's akhara.'

He spoke in a gentle but decisive tone. It had been quite some time since Reba had visited and she was not expecting to go again, especially on an empty stomach.

'No, Dadu, I cannot exercise now. I have just finished school and my stomach is growling,' she replied.

She thought of the weights and the yoga poses she had

---

[57] Rakshit, 'The Sport of Elephant Lifting', 253-264.

seen. It would be too much work for her to manage now after a long day of study.

A compromise was in order.

'Okay,' her grandfather replied, 'eat some banana and bread to gain some energy and stamina.'

'Banana and bread,' she said. 'Then I will be ready.'

Reba realized that there was no changing his mind, so she relented.

After eating, Reba walked with her *dadu* towards Ghosh's akhara. The afternoon was fading into evening. As they walked, each storefront that they passed revealed a different world. A printing press chugged and a skinny man with smudged hands gathered and stacked the pages; in another, four sewing machines spun as the tailors turned long, brightly coloured bolts of cloth into sarees. On the sidewalk itself, vendors sat beside their goods, ready to satisfy the crowds as they returned home from work. Sacks of rice, piles of bitter melon and pyramids of green coconuts were ready to quench the evening hunger and thirst. As they walked down the busy sidewalk, slipping between the hasty motorcycles and the plodding cow, Reba wondered what her first lesson would be like.

Finally, as they passed through the open gates of the college the gatekeeper motioned them up the stairs. They climbed up the two flights of stairs, one long and one short, until they stood inside the lobby. Just then Ghosh appeared.

'Why didn't you come sooner?' he demanded. 'So many days have passed!'

Had he been expecting her sooner? Had her grandfather arranged the visit? Or did Ghosh just *know* when she would return. Ghosh was treating her as if she were already a valued member of the school; as if she were one of them.

Her grandfather interrupted her thoughts and said, 'Reba, he asked you a question.'

'I saw the big muscles, sir, and all the men doing bodybuilding,' Reba said. 'Will I become just like them if I train here?'

Ghosh smiled and said, '*Na, na*! How can a woman's figure be like that? I will teach you yoga. Come with me.'

Without waiting for Reba's response, he shot through a small door opposite his office and disappeared into the main yoga room where the men usually practised. Reba's grandfather motioned emphatically for her to follow Ghosh and she did.

'Reba! Listen.'

Ghosh's words were commanding, clear and concise. She hurried to catch up with him. 'Your health will either compel you to live the life of an old woman or permit you to enjoy the munificent beautiful gifts of God in this wonderful world even when you are old!'[58]

Reba just stared back, feeling unsure and small in his presence. She nodded her head gently.

Ghosh continued. 'It is very difficult to carry out good intentions in daily life—but health being of primary importance, the good habits of health must be carried out. Let's begin.'[59]

He took a small step to the side to allow her to pass, and pointed towards a pile of blue cushions that were rolled up against the wall. 'Take one.'

Reba walked past him, crossing the shiny red floor of the big, empty room. She picked the cushion that was closest to her, unrolled it on the floor, sat down and looked at Ghosh.

---

[58] Bishnu Ghosh, *Yoga Cure* (Self-published: 1961), 2.
[59] Ibid.

'*Shavasana*!' he said sharply. 'Lie on your back.'

She lay down, positioned her head towards the *byayamacharya* and stretched her legs. The air blew in through the window, making the curtains ripple in the wind.

'Now, Reba, you must completely relax your limbs. This is very important because this is the Corpse Pose.'

Reba lay perfectly still, staring up at the ceiling fans that turned slowly in the warm evening. Byayamacharya Ghosh's next command interrupted her stillness.

'*Pavanamuktasana*! Wind-Relieving Posture. Bring your right thigh against your abdomen. Hold your leg with your hands. Press it tight.'

Combined with her determination, excitement and nervousness, Reba did just that.

'Breathe, Reba. Do not hold your breath.'

Ghosh said a little more gently. She let her breath exit slowly.

'Good, Reba. Breath control is very important. You will need that for your stunts.'

Stunts! *What about yoga*? Stunts seemed like a different path from the health-focused approach of yoga. But Reba, free-spirited and adventurous as she was, felt excited about the prospect of performing stunts.

'Release your right leg.'

Ghosh paused briefly while it moved.

'Now left leg. Press it against your abdomen. Stretch out your right leg.' He continued, without missing a beat.

'Left leg down. Both legs!'

Ghosh settled into a rhythm, his instructions clear and precise.

'Maintain the posture and breathe.'

Reba's breath moved in and out while she held her knees tightly to her chest.

'Now stretch both your legs and relax in Shavasana.'

Ghosh made Reba perform a couple of exercises and discharged her.

Reba left Ghosh's college that evening full of excitement and hyper-aware of her breathing and body movements. Her grandfather was waiting for her outside the akhara. She eagerly rushed to tell him about all that transpired.

'Dadu, the first positions were quite easy but they need to be mastered for health. The Wind-Relieving Posture must be done for the digestive system.'

She was practically skipping in glee as she spoke. Her grandfather tried to keep pace with her stride and her stories.

'Reba, you are learning so much. Good for you.'

'Then we did the Cobra and the Bow postures. But the stretching posture was the best.'

The moon was rising in the sky as they returned home.

Her grandfather finally asked when she slowed down.

'Shall I too learn yoga? What do you think, Reba?'

'Oh yes, Dadu, and I will teach you!'

They both chuckled, but Reba paused and said, 'But Dadu, maybe it's best you don't do the stunts.'

'The stunts? What do you mean, Reba?'

'I don't know yet. But next I am to learn the stunts!'

Her grandfather frowned and thought to himself: *Is this true? Aren't stunts dangerous? What's with young people with stars in their eyes? Yoga sounds safe and healthy. It will take her far in life ...*

Reba continued to attend Ghosh's college in the afternoons after school.

As soon as her classes got over, she would quickly exit school and walk straight to Ghosh's college with a great deal of eagerness. Her afternoons were spent developing her body, but during the day she spent time developing her mind.

Reba was not just an average student at Ghosh's college. She was being trained to teach one day. She was learning how to do the postures, but in time would come to know how to use yoga to cure many diseases and ailments. This was all part of the Yoga Cure Institute, a section of Ghosh's college that focused entirely on therapeutic yoga. She was energetic and a natural leader—necessary traits of any teacher at Ghosh's college. Most importantly, she was being trained by Byayamacharya Bishnu Charan Ghosh personally.

As her time under Ghosh's instruction continued, she would learn about asanas for agility and how to take care of people suffering from polio, rickets or obesity. Yoga could help in gastric troubles like chronic dysentery and constipation; insomnia or varicose veins.[60]

'Yoga,' Ghosh often said, 'teaches you to shake off stress and strain, both nervous and muscular, and even of the brain, quickly before damage is done to your system and your immunity to disease is destroyed.'[61] Anyone who did not believe him was encouraged to test his teaching. Any doubt on validity was met with confidence. 'If you are suffering, contact me. Let me prove the truth in my statement!'

---

[60] Ibid., 3–4.
[61] Ibid., 2.

All this amounted to hogwash if it were not for the many stories and personal accounts from those he had healed. Ghosh's ability to heal people and develop successful athletes was well known throughout the neighbourhood. Reba knew that many of his star students had come from nothing, but within a few months under Ghosh's able guidance they were transformed, thrust into a new world of performance, competition and teaching. This allowed them to make a living, support their families and maybe even travel to faraway lands. She met some of the very people she had heard so much about, like Monotosh Roy, Kamal Bandhari, Shanti Dutta, all the 'strong men' people were talking about.

These men were training to take on the world. They had accepted Ghosh as their guru and almost put their lives in his hands. Since Ghosh was their guru, he would lead them from *darkness* to *light*. *Gu* stands for darkness, ignorance and *ru* stands for complete annihilation. He was both their spiritual guide and teacher to whom full obedience was expected.[62]

And the relationship was deep.

As Reba thought about these star students at Ghosh's college, she wondered, *Am I next?*

---

[62] M.K. Raina, 'Guru-Shishya Relationship in Indian Culture: The Possibility of a Creative Resilient Framework', *Psychology and Developing Societies* 14, no. 1 (2002), 167–98.

7

Bishnu Charan Ghosh—the Making of a Legend

How the Leading Exponent of Yoga Changed Lives

Bishnu Charan Ghosh was a living legend by the time Reba met him. At a time when people needed strength and the city needed entertainment, gymnasiums became the centres of culture and pride in Bengal. A few were more political than others, but they were all changing the face of the culture. Ghosh and his akhara were creating highly successful students and making headlines overseas. He was known for taking orphans and destitutes and turning them into stars. He could identify with them because his childhood was full of profound loss.

Bishnu was the youngest of eight children. His father Bhagabati Charan Ghosh came from the small village of Ichhapur, north of Calcutta. Bhagabati was the eldest son of a schoolteacher who had succumbed to smallpox, leaving the care of the family and management of the finances to Bhagabati.[63]

Bhagabati struggled to make ends meet; he was also faced with the task of repaying a loan of 50 rupees[64] that his father had taken before his death. He was forced to sell his mother's pair of silver bangles, but even that failed to cover the debt. The financial hardship and difficulties of his childhood shaped Bhagabati greatly. He developed a strong work ethic and a belief in the value of education. After taking a job in the Public Works Department in Rangoon (modern-day Yangon), he returned to Calcutta and married Gyana Prabha, who would become Bishnu's mother.[65]

One day, Bhagabati was walking with a co-worker along a wooded roadway when they came upon a field. The sun was casting its rays on the grass when a peaceful figure appeared and spoke to Bhagabati. The figure was Lahiri Mahasaya a disciple of the great Babaji. The vision was enough to convince Bhagabati to take initiation into Kriya Yoga. During that time, Bhagabati and Gyana were expecting their fourth child. The very evening, they departed for Benares.

Once there, they found Lahiri Mahasaya seated in meditation with his legs crossed in *Padmasana*. They bowed down before him to receive initiation. Together, Bhagabati and Gyana became yogis.

---

[63] Sri Sananda Lal Ghosh, *Mejda* (Kolkata: Yogoda Satsanga Society of India, 1980), 6.
[64] There are no records of inflation of the rupee until 1958. Fifty rupees in 1958 is about 4,500 rupees in 2022. https://www.in2013dollars.com/india/inflation
[65] Ghosh, *Mejda*, 12.

Bhagabati later told his children that Lahiri Mahasaya prophesied, 'My daughter, through the grace of God your son will be a prophet. He will show mankind the way to God realization. Through his life and teachings, many people will slough off the delusions of this world and find salvation. You travelled here by train. You saw how the engine pulled the cars; in the same manner, your son will draw souls from the ordinary to the divine sphere.'[66]

Shortly thereafter, on 5 January 1893, Gyana gave birth to Mukunda Lal who became Paramahansa Yogananda.

Bishnu Charan Ghosh was born a decade later on 24 June 1903 in Lahore where Bhagabati was serving as the deputy examiner in the Office of Railway Accounts of the North-Western Railway.[67]

Gyana was a loving and affectionate mother, with a heart that was big enough to hold the love for all her eight children, her husband and countless others beyond her family. She was a talented sculptor, making statues of deities like Kali; a cook par excellence and, an outstanding teacher to her children teaching them manners, virtues and scriptures.[68]

Less than a year after Ghosh's birth, many relatives gathered in Calcutta to celebrate the wedding of Ghosh's eldest brother. Despite the festivities and the feeling of celebration in the air, Gyana felt uneasy about the future.[69]

The Asiatic cholera pandemic was ravaging South Asia in full force.[70] Its first wave had begun in the early nineteenth

---

[66] Ibid., 16–17.
[67] Ibid., 44.
[68] Ibid., 46–47.
[69] Ibid., 52–53.
[70] Asiatic Cholera Pandemic of 1817–23. http://www.ph.ucla.edu/epi/

century. Although the early cases were found in Bihar in 1816, the pandemic was thought to have started not too far from Calcutta before spreading to nearly every Asian country. In 1837, there was another resurgence of cholera in Bengal which reached up to Afghanistan. Then in the 1840s, the disease was transported along the shipping routes as far away as China, with another branch reaching towards modern-day Iran via the Caspian Sea. By the 1850s, the cholera was also ravaging Europe as well as North and South America.[71] By the time the deadly disease showed up in Bengal a century later, it was a well-known killer.

During the wedding celebrations, the bride fell ill with cholera. Gyana nursed her with care, but the young woman could not be saved.[72] The deadly disease was just too powerful. Gyana fell seriously ill as well and passed away on 26 April 1904.

Gyana's eldest son, who had lost both his fiancée and mother, was grief-stricken. As Bhagabati held Mukunda tightly in sorrow, Mukunda screamed, 'Release me! Release me! I will get her, I will bring her back!'

Although he was a spiritual person with a deep sense of prophecy, he was simply a heartbroken young boy who suffered great loss. Bhagabati was too shocked to say anything. He slowly became aware that now he was a widower with eight motherless children. Ghosh was barely a year old then.[73]

According to legend, the Ghosh family's ancestry can be traced back to the eleventh century when Makaranda Ghosh,

---

snow/pandemic1817-23.html
[71] Asiatic Cholera Pandemic of 1846–63. http://www.ph.ucla.edu/epi/snow/pandemic1846-63.html
[72] Ghosh, 53.
[73] Ibid., 54.

part of the Kayastha caste known for scribal or literary duties, was invited by King Adisur to settle in Bengal.[74] This legend is a controversial one which played a pivotal role in the history of Bengal as a whole.

Around the turn of the twentieth century, as the sons and daughters of Bharat Mata were increasingly committed to winning independence from their colonizers, India's unique traditions became more important. Because Indians could build their national identity around these traditions. In a way, their past was being built just as much as their future. Of course, India was a land with millennia of traditions, but the British made some of these traditions into unacceptable acts. So the Bengali literati sprang into action to create a *proper* history of India, which included a heated debate about the 'controversial' King Adisur.[75]

According to legend, King Adisur had invited five spiritually pure Brahmins to move from Kannauj to Bengal in order to re-purify the area which was seen to be suffering spiritually under the influence of Buddhism.[76] Thus in Bengal, a 'purer' line of succession could emerge, one which informed Bengal's social structure. These Brahmins eventually settled in Bengal and called themselves Kulin Brahmins signifying a noble origin.

However, many viewed this story with great scepticism as there was no material evidence that proved the existence of the king.[77]

---

[74] Kumkum Chatterjee, 'The King of Controversy: History and Nation-Making in Late Colonial India,' *The American Historical Review* 110, no. 5 (2005), 1455-56.
[75] Ibid., 1455.
[76] Ibid., 175.
[77] Ibid., 1463.

However, others argued that *belief* in the legend of King Adisur did inform the culture regardless of its empirical truth.[78] His story told over centuries had become an inextricable part of the culture of Bengal. According to this argument, history is the culture of the people and their understanding of heritage. So, from the viewpoint of Bengalis, King Adisur was part of the land, culture and history of Bengal. This was their history and any attempt to discredit it by 'outside' methods of analysis would only further alienate a culture from their own history.

With the loss of his mother, Ghosh grew up with a piece of his heart missing; the piece of a heart that knows a mother's love and care; the piece that develops with a feeling of comfort and acceptance. What grew in its place was a deep sense of empathy with orphans and others who had been badly bruised by life's brutal sleight of hand.

Ghosh's teens and early twenties were greatly impacted by the pioneering spirit of Mukunda whose life had also changed course with the death of his mother. And it was a spiritual calling that led him forward. He committed his life to the tradition of Kriya Yoga, took the vows of *sannyasa* and became Swami Yogananda. He left India in 1920 for the US. For fifteen years Yogananda travelled and taught in the West, establishing himself as a significant teacher of Kriya Yoga while learning the ways of America.

The American yoga circuit served as a platform for Ghosh as well. In 1939, Ghosh left for Europe and the United States with his star pupil Buddha Bose. Along with Swami Yogananda, they travelled much of the Western world displaying both the spiritual and physical aspects of yoga.

---

[78] Ibid., 1455-56.

Throughout their travels, Buddha Bose was the star performer, as it was not customary for the guru to demonstrate. While Ghosh explained the various asanas to crowds of curious attendees, Buddha would twist and fold his beautiful, young body in demonstration.

The two men were close. Ghosh had invested heavily in Buddha's training and cared for him deeply, much like he would for Reba a few years later. It was this care and training in yoga that pulled Buddha out of his own unfortunate childhood situation. Buddha, like Ghosh, had grown up without his mother.

Buddha's parents were magicians who had tried their luck on the British circus stage. His father Rajah had seen a magician as a child growing up in Burma (modern-day Myanmar) and became obsessed with the art. While he was in England, a Miss Emmie Johnson caught his eye.[79] She became his stage hand, appearing as part of his act. Soon they fell deeply in love, had a baby girl and left England for India. Their second child, Buddha, was born en route on the *SS Derflinger*. When the liner was making its way across the Arabian Sea, Francis Joseph Chandra Bose, *daknam* 'Buddha', was born sometime before it docked in Colombo, Ceylon (modern-day Sri Lanka).[80]

Once they arrived in Calcutta, Rajah and Emmie and their two children lived at the Great Eastern Hotel. But every morning, Rajah would leave his family and disappear into the northern part of the city. After a little while, it became clear that something was amiss. Rajah had a Bengali wife whom he was hiding from Emmie. Then on 16 May 1914, two more

---

[79] Jerome Armstrong, *Calcutta Yoga* (New Delhi: Macmillan, 2020), 3.
[80] Ibid., 13.

children were born. Emmie welcomed a new son, Buddha's younger brother. On that same day, Rajah welcomed another baby, the firstborn son of his Bengali wife.[81]

Emmie refused to tolerate the situation any more, so she decided to return to England. But she did not have the money to pay for a ticket. Disowned from her own British family for marrying an Indian, she was stranded. She struck a deal with her father-in-law that would have a profound impact on young Buddha's life. Her father-in-law would pay for her ticket to England as long as she left one of his grandchildren behind. Unable to fathom leaving a girl or an infant, by the process of elimination she left behind Buddha.[82]

Buddha was too young to understand the decision of his mother, but it did not stop him from chasing any white woman he saw on the streets of Calcutta. With tears streaming down his cheeks, he would cry out, 'Mama!'

Ghosh easily understood the trauma of a young boy who lost his mother. He accepted the young Buddha into his akhara. Once Buddha met Ghosh, the void that was created by the loss of his family would be filled by the creation of a new one. Eventually, Buddha married Ghosh's daughter Ava Rani.

Reba's young life was not very different from Ghosh's and Buddha's. She too was displaced as a child, separated from her parents for long periods of time. Ghosh could deeply connect with those who had lost their identities in some way. Most of his students truly knew what loss was. They left their homes as Reba had; they lost their family, language and culture. And many had very little left to lose when they started training

---

[81] Ibid., 24.
[82] Ibid., 25.

under Ghosh. They hoped that he would transform their talent into a lifelong successful career.

Ghosh's worldwide success and his outstanding performances in the West with Buddha and Yogananda rippled through Calcutta. There were rumours that he had been photographed for newspapers, performed for admiring audiences, which included academics and military leaders, and was lauded as 'the leading exponent of yoga' as far away as Washington, DC. Calcuttans were extremely proud of their neighbour.

The rumours were all true.[83]

But Ghosh was more than just a legendary world traveller. He had a way of healing the people he worked with, sometimes pulling them off the street and giving them a new life. His claims of using yoga to cure polio, dysentery and even hysteria, were true more often than not. From the simplest therapeutic yoga exercises to the most dangerous and exciting stunts, Ghosh mastered everything. Once when Reba's nephew Swapan suffered from tonsillitis, Ghosh prescribed him a cure and Swapan never had an issue with his tonsils again.[84]

The World War II was raging when Ghosh and Buddha returned to Calcutta following their travels abroad. Surrounding Ghosh's college were constant reminders of war and the simmering demands of Indian nationalism. Millions perished in the Bengal Famine of 1943; hundreds of

---

[83] This is constructed based on the author's interviews with those in the neighbourhood of the akhara. Nearly everyone who is old enough to know of Ghosh remembers him clearly.

[84] Author's interview with Swapan Talukdar on 16 October 2019. He said, 'It is a cure, I'm convinced! To this day, I've never had a problem.' At the time of the interview, Swapan was seventy-three years old.

thousands of Hindus and Muslims massacred each other in a fight to assume power after the exit of the British. Death and desperation were present and palpable.

At the conclusion of the war, while much of the world collectively heaved a sigh of relief, India stood waiting. She was ready to be free, but freedom came at a cost for her. She would be divided into two countries—India and Pakistan. While many returned home after the conclusion of the war, including the oppressor Britain herself, residents of the Indian subcontinent waited to learn where their home should be. Finally when India gained Independence, millions were displaced in one of the largest human migrations in recorded history.

8

Fractured Freedom for India—the Partition of 1947

More Independence for Its Women

On 15 August 1947 when India finally gained Independence from the British Empire, Comilla was no longer in India; now it was in East Pakistan (modern-day Bangladesh). Freedom came at a heavy price for a lot of people. As the land of East and West Pakistan was now a country of Islam, Hindus who found themselves there fled to India. Muslims who found themselves in India fled to either east or west. It is believed that Partition displaced more than fifteen million people who found themselves on the wrong side of the border.

Partition was arranged hastily after the World War II by the departing British.

Any hope for a thoughtful process was injected with urgency when Prime Minister of Great Britain Clement Attlee said, 'It is important that all the above processes be completed as quickly as possible.' So during the hot and stormy monsoon months of 1947, as India raced towards Independence, the borders of the new homelands were drawn using a set of outdated maps, with often misaligned goals and *as quickly as possible*.

Borders have been drawn and redrawn over the course of human history. While conquering kings and warriors have shaped their newly won territory, they usually adapted their boundaries to work hand in hand with the natural barriers of mountains, valleys, rivers and oceans.[85]

In India, the regions affected by Partition were populated by millions of people who shared a culture, history and a language. Their ancestors too had shared language and culture, and had shifted gradually around the subcontinent to settle in natural ways that made sense for human survival. They had sufficient water to sustain them; they cultivated crops and animals; they were located near profitable trade routes. Their cities arose over time, as did their shrines, sacred sites and homes.

But Partition did not take into account the natural landmarks, shared economic resources, shared language or culture. The primary consideration was consolidation of political power, which meant that religious belief came to the forefront. These lands, like most centres of human development, were occupied by those who spoke the same language but differed in religious belief. These countries were assigned a nationality based only on religion and political leanings. Cities were assigned to their new countries. In short, centuries of human civilization and development were upended with the hasty stroke of a bureaucrat's pen.

---

[85] Thapar, *Early India,* 39.

Fractured Freedom for India—the Partition of 1947 71

Even if Indian West Bengal contained less actual land and a smaller population than East Pakistan, they were satisfied if the political consolidation was to their advantage. East Pakistan, in turn, gave away all the tea in Darjeeling and all the water in the Hooghly to get a state in which they could achieve political dominance.[86] If less land made for a more stable political future, so be it. But in the new India, West Bengal's stability would prove to be difficult because it now lacked sufficient rice production to feed its population. And it lacked jute production, a vital economic resource that was now primarily across the border in East Pakistan, while most of the jute mills were located in West Bengal.

These issues of Partition were not limited to the political and economic concerns of Bengal. They spanned all of the borders, reaching end to end across the two countries as they tried to become independent not only from the British, but also from each other. Their fortunes had been inextricably intertwined for millennia and now they had to pull themselves apart in a matter of months, like the unweaving of a detailed rug. Practical matters like visas, passports and currency needed to be sorted out. The new nation of Pakistan was left without its own bank notes for months following Partition. Without a currency of their own—with the only mint printing notes in India—Pakistan had to use Indian banknotes until midway through 1948.[87]

As the boundaries were drawn, West Bengal became Hindu majority now. Leaders expected that the eleven

---

[86] Joya Chatterji, *The Spoils of Partition* (Cambridge, UK: Cambridge University Press, 2007), 55–56.

[87] Urvashi Butalia. *The Other Side of Silence* (Durham, North Carolina: Duke University Press, 2000, Part 4).

million Hindus who found themselves in East Pakistan would be content in their new country, as would the five million Muslims in West Bengal.[88]

Absolutely no one expected mass migration.

With the birth of the two countries, ordinary people tried to figure out what freedom meant while fracturing into two pieces.[89] Quickly, millions realized that they could not possibly remain on the wrong side of the border. Although they were newly freed from Britain's reign, this fractured freedom was not enough. The fear of living as part of a religious and political minority was too much to bear. So over the course of five months between August and December 1947, around 15 million people crossed over the western border between India and Pakistan.[90] And over the next two decades five million more moved between East and West Bengal in one of the largest human migrations in recorded history.

Most of them walked.

Trains, roads and waterways became overwhelmed by a swollen river of people passing between the old country and the new. The *kafila*s trailed to the horizon in both directions, far ahead into the unknown, the future; and far back into the distance, the past. Many carried a brick from their home tucked in their belongings. But bricks are heavy, so others just put handfuls of the earth in their pockets, determined to bring a piece of their homeland with them to their new country.

Families walked together.

---

[88] Chatterji, *The Spoils of Partition*, 57.
[89] Stuart Roberts, 'A Tryst with Destiny', University of Cambridge. https://www.cam.ac.uk/tryst_with_destiny
[90] Chatterji, *The Spoils of Partition*, 105.

Children carried even smaller children so that their fathers could balance the bed frame on their heads. Carts overflowed with items, all tied down with rope. When late monsoon rains drenched the travellers, they tried to get underneath the carts at each stop along the way to avoid the *jhom jhom kore brishti* and stay dry, if only for a few moments. They squatted in the water, barefoot, trying to find shelter. Many carts and cars were overloaded with possessions. Atop the vehicles were trunks; atop the trunks were more people. Once there was no room for even one more body, a child was lifted up and passed to someone atop the truck. There was always room for one more, so long as they were small.[91]

Often the endless caravans of migrants of people flowed in opposite directions side by side, like a great highway whose speeding traffic was only separated by an imaginary line drawn down the centre. The atmosphere between the two religious groups became increasingly hostile. The situation was especially horrific for women who were used as a tool against the enemy. Once they were *dirtied,* deformed or impregnated by the other side, they became exiles from their own families. Rape was a weapon that could eliminate the enemy by rendering them *impure*. Each family responded differently to this threat. Some killed their women so that dishonour could not be brought upon the family. Some took their chances and were met with luck. Others lost their women in fatal attacks. Some families sent their women off ahead of the rest in an attempt to get them across the border for a better chance of safety.

Reba and Jyotsna had moved from Comilla to Calcutta three years before Independence, so they had no trauma of

---

[91] 'The Road to Partition', https://www.nationalarchives.gov.uk/

migration. They had growing connections to the city. Besides their uncle, there was Jyotsna's new husband, Manmatha who had studied at Dacca University. After finishing his study of science at Vidyasagar College, Calcutta, he took a job. During that period, he rented a house in the far south of Calcutta with an ancient look and a large courtyard.[92] Eventually, he retired as the official superintendent of the Department of Civil Supplies, Government of West Bengal.

After Partition, Reba's parents migrated from Comilla and settled in Rishra about twenty kilometres from Calcutta.

Reba helped take care of her nephew Swapan. Jyotsna was doing the best she could to care for her son, but there was nothing anyone could do to prevent the sound of people being murdered in the streets from seeping deep into the memory of even babies.

In the hot Calcutta streets, the air was thick with the chants of *Hare Krishna* and *Allahu Akbar*, and often interrupted by the unbelievably haunting shrieks that emerged in the moments before murder. Only a few months old, it would not seem possible for Swapan to store a memory in his mind, but this was a time that defied logic and memory. The memories buried themselves deep in the hearts of all the beings who lived through it.

Those settled in India settled into their new homes in a new country with a new identity and a new purpose, and were left to grapple with the practical problem of how to make ends meet. How would families find comfort and peace once again? How would they engage with the new identities of their country? How could daily life look *normal* once

---

[92] Author interview with Swapan Talukdar, 15 October 2019.

again? The answers to these questions were worked out day after day.

If they made it safely across the frontier and into the unknown new world, the lives of women changed substantially. No longer would the previous *normal* patterns of life dictate their futures. Domestic and professional roles were broadly reinterpreted. Gender roles were reinvented. Women were thrust into the public sphere in ways that would have been previously unheard of. If anyone in the family had the capacity to support their loved ones in this new environment, they were obligated to go forth. Reba, like many other women, started working. While there was still some affinity for earlier notions of womanhood, a modern woman was emerging. The desperation for resettlement encouraged the change. Partition destroyed so much of the past, while reshaping the future.[93]

---

[93] Butalia, *The Other Side of Silence*, Part 4.

Ghosh And Reba—
Building a Relationship

9

Bishnu Charan Ghosh's Star Pupils

'The Guru Is the Father, the Guru Is the Mother, the Guru Is God'

Byayamacharya Bishnu Charan Ghosh was Reba's guru, but he was more than that. For thousands of years, success in yoga had required deep dedication to the guru. One traditional text of Hatha Yoga, the *Shiva Samhita*, explains the relationship:

> Now I shall teach how to quickly succeed in yoga. Yogis who know this, do not fail when practising yoga. If it comes from the guru's mouth, wisdom is potent. If it does not, it is barren and impotent and brings great suffering. He who zealously makes his guru happy and practices his teachings quickly gains the reward of those teachings. The guru is the father, the guru is the mother, the guru is God. In this, there is no doubt. For this reason, disciples serve him with

their actions, thoughts and words. Everything that is good for the self is obtained through the grace of the guru, so the guru is to be served constantly or else no good will happen.[94]

The first mark of success in yoga is that the practitioner must believe in their heart of hearts that practice will bear fruit. Reba had complete faith in Byayamacharya because she had seen many of his students become very successful. One must not only put in the effort, but also have faith in the power of practice. Reba was diligently practising and believing in the path. She was devoted to her guru, just like her mother was to Ramakrishna. Having faith is the second mark of success.

Third, importantly, is honouring one's guru. Beyond this a sense of equanimity is important along with restraint of the senses and discipline in diet.[95] The *Hatha Yoga Pradipika*, the fifteenth-century central Sanskrit text on Hatha Yoga, states, 'The fool who wishes to master yoga otherwise, without the process of yoga initiation (*yogadiksa*) and without a guru, does not obtain success, even after billions of eons.'[96]

A guru was necessary for success in yoga. Therefore, the disciple had a sense of duty towards the guru. Without the guru, success was absolutely impossible.

Repayment for something great must be matched in greatness. In this sense, the disciple owed everything to the guru. Just as the *Shiva Samhita* stated, the guru was father,

---

[94] *Shiva Samhita*, 3.10–4, in *Roots of Yoga*, eds James Mallinson and Mark Singleton (Penguin Random House UK, 2017), 68.
[95] *Shiva Samhita*, 3.19–20 in ibid., 69.
[96] *Hatha Yoga Pradipika*, 1.38–9 in ibid., 70.

mother and God. This type of devotion and dedication was deeply ingrained in the process of initiation.

Repayment to the guru is central to the story of Ekalavya. The story is one of indebtedness and an ode to the proper way in which the guru–disciple relationship should unfold.[97]

As Ghosh trained more and more students, many of them had success. He had a way of healing, inspiring and truly changing the course of his students' lives. Talent, faith and practice all intersected in various ways depending on the student.

As Reba was developing her skills and Buddha Bose was growing in prominence, there were other students showing promise. Labanya Palit, another female student, was mastering asanas and also doing motorcycle stunts. She was beginning to think about writing yoga instructions for other women. How would women learn yoga if nearly nothing was directed towards them? With Ghosh's blessings, she began writing extensive columns about asana for women in the local Bengali paper *Jugantar*. She demonstrated asanas and wrote about how and why women should take up the practice.

Gouri Shankar Mukerji was another upcoming talent. He attended a show with the Gemini Circus and met Ghosh for the first time there.[98] Ghosh spotted his potential when they met, but Mukerji was not keen to take up physical culture since he had a scientific bent of mind and wanted to focus on his studies instead. Then he met Ghosh again in 1944, shortly after the tragic death of the latter's oldest son Srikrishna.

---

[97] S. Shankar, 'The Thumb of Ekalavya: Postcolonial Studies and the "Third World" Scholar in a Neocolonial World', *World Literature Today* 68, no. 3, Summer (1994), 481–82.
[98] Armstrong, *Calcutta Yoga*, 273.

Mukerji was struggling deeply with asthma and Ghosh agreed to meet with him despite the personal grief he was facing. There was something about Mukerji that reminded him of his son, and Ghosh took him into his gym and his heart.

Mukerji went on to work side by side with Reba for some years. He would kneel by her side as the motorcycle flung over her chest, carefully attending to the stunt. Eventually, Mukerji left for Germany, trained in medicine and wrote about the scientific effects of asanas and pranayama. Later in his life, he returned to Calcutta and served as Ghosh's personal doctor and a close confidant.

Monotosh Roy also saw great success under Ghosh's tutelage. He recalled later in his life that it was the initiation by his guru that changed him. Roy would sit in Ghosh's presence with shivers coursing up and down his spine and eyes and ears completely focused on every word coming from his guru's mouth. Through initiation, the secrets of muscle control were instilled in him.[99] Ghosh told him to have faith, to believe, to work every day with determination and belief in the process. Without steadfast commitment, the devil will make his home in the heart.[100]

Shortly after his initiation, Roy won the first Mr Universe title for India in 1951 by winning the World Bodybuilding Championship. This reconfirmed what the community already knew—Ghosh's College of Physical Education created legends.

---

[99] Ibid., 274.
[100] Ibid.

10

Reba—the New Woman

Becoming Strong in a Focused, Calm Way

The path between Reba's school and Ghosh's college was a straight one. If the day was not too hot, she would love to walk in the sun. After a day in the classroom, it was wonderful to feel the warmth on her face and shoulders. As she got closer to Ghosh's college she passed iron shops, coconut stands and sweet shops. Occasionally, the heat of cooking spices from the street vendors burned her nose, her eyes watering as she walked. She made sure to eat a banana or a small piece of bread, so that she had enough energy for her afternoon practice. But she performed best when her stomach was mostly empty as a large meal would make her feel sluggish. So, she would save that for after the yoga practice.

One day, Reba quickly walked through the gate of Ghosh's college and went up to the first floor and peeked into Byayamacharya's office like she did daily. When he was not on the ground floor with the weightlifters, he would often sit in the office behind the heavy wooden desk, no doubt planning the next performance of his students. She turned left and walked down the hall, slipping off her sandals before entering the large, open women's yoga room. She set down her school bag by the door and went to the centre of the room. The floor was the colour of dried sage. When the sunlight came in through the windows on the opposite wall, the entire room glowed a gentle, cosy green. The ceiling fans whirred as she wiped beads of sweat from her brow, the afternoon heat making itself known. Dressed in her loose clothing, she began her practice.

She began with deep breathing.

This she knew would give her power and energy. She stood very tall, her feet placed under her hips for alignment, her spine upright. She started to breathe, six counts in, six counts out. Six counts in, six counts out. Big, deep breaths, ten times in a row. As she inhaled, she reached her arms up towards the ceiling, stretching even taller. As she filled her lungs with air, her ribs widened as the air passed through her nostrils. Then she exhaled slowly. She lowered her arms until they were by her sides at the same time that her lungs emptied. Her ribs compressed in as she pushed the breath from her body.

Breath by breath, slow inhales followed by slow exhales.

Six counts in, six counts out.

She could feel the muscles between her ribs becoming stronger, her mind becoming clearer and more focused. Her body started to heat up, this time from the inside out. Another bead of sweat formed. This type of heat she knew had power in it. This was the type of heat the yogis talk about. Strength, determination, focus, *tapas*.

After she finished the breathing exercise, she continued with her asanas. Next, she focused on the spine. It was crucial to keep it flexible. It needed to be bent side to side, front to back. It needed to be twisted. This was not your average exercise routine. This was *yoga byayam*, a combination of yoga and exercise. Normal exercise routines could keep the body healthy but they could not revive injured parts. It was only yoga byayam that would heal the ailing parts of the body. The asanas followed by Shavasana made the whole body function properly, resulting in its natural processes working to their full potential.[101]

Next was side bending, the exercise version of *Ardha Chandrasana*.

She moved her spine to the right as she exhaled, counting *1*. Then back to the middle as she inhaled, standing upright with her back straight, *2*. To the left as she exhaled, *3*. Then back to the middle, *4*. She repeated this steady and intentional movement until her count reached *10*. Standing still for a few moments before repeating the exercise, she felt the fog in her mind from her day of schoolwork lifting. After her side-bends were complete, she moved her spine forward and back with the Back Arching Toe Touching Exercise. Again she took a breath into her chest, this time with her arms up towards the ceiling as she bent her spine backwards. As she exhaled, she folded forward touching her hands to the floor and her forehead to her knees. Inhale, reaching up and back. Exhale, bending forward. With each repetition, she felt herself full of vigour as any tension she had carried during the day dissipated.

---

[101] Reba Rakshit, 'Where Is the Final Destination in Byayam? *Byayam Charcha*. Exact issue unknown.

The first part of her exercise programme was filled with these therapeutic yoga exercises, where she moved her body as she breathed. Now as she finished them, she moved on to the asanas. These were more difficult; they required stillness. It was one thing to be strong while moving, but entirely another to be strong while holding still. Holding the body in strenuous positions could make the mind run wild, but Reba knew that controlling the mind was key to controlling the body.

'If you can control the mind, the results are all within reach,' Byayamacharya would say whenever he saw her mind wandering or whenever she had lost concentration. He had taught her—just as a car can be controlled by the clutch, the body can be controlled by the mind.[102]

'Slow the mind down, make it suspend its action just as a car does when it slows out of gear to the point before it stalls. The power is not lost. In fact, it is brought under control. Like this, control the body with the mind. This type of careful control is karmic action in motion. Joy or sorrow, it is all in your hands. Good health is there for the taking.'[103]

Standing tall, Reba focused her mind, then her body.

Balancing the forehead to knee was next.

She pressed her left foot down into the hard tile floor, balancing on her heel. She lifted her right knee up towards her chest and held her right foot with both hands. Balancing on her left leg, straight and strong, she slowly stretched her right leg forward, straightening the knee. Her legs made a perfect ninety degree angle. She paused,

---

[102] Ibid.
[103] Ibid.

took a breath, focusing her eyes and concentrating her mind. The next part was the hardest. Moving very slowly, she rounded her spine forward over her right leg until her face was close to her leg. Finally, she tucked her chin and touched her forehead to her right knee. She wobbled a little but maintained her focus. She took a slow, steady breath. There she stood motionless, in perfect balance. The entire world stopped for a moment as she concentrated with her whole body and mind. Then, just as carefully as she entered the pose, she exited, standing up and setting her right foot on the floor next to the left.

She came back to stillness. She stood, feeling both feet underneath her while a wave of relaxation flushed through her body, wiping away the posture from her cells.

After balancing out her body, side to side, she unrolled a thin blue mattress on the floor. She lay down on her belly and stretched her long legs behind her. Now she would bend her spine, practising making it supple and strong.

Dhanurasana, the Bow Posture.

She bent her knees, reaching back to catch her feet in her hands. Taking a deep breath into her chest, she kicked her feet up high behind her while bending her spine backwards. She looked up, reaching her chin up, stretching the whole front side of her body. Her body looked like an archer's bow, drawn tight. Time nearly stopped as she held in stillness, her mind alert but relaxed. Precise but calm. Then she relaxed down, let go of her feet and turned her left cheek so it rested on the mattress, letting the pulse of her heartbeat thump against the floor.

She moved from back-bending into stretching postures. Pushing herself up from the mattress, she sat down on it, stretching her legs straight forward in front of her.

Paschimottanasana.

She reached forward and held her toes with her hands, then folded forward, draping her body over her legs. Her head rested on her knees, her back lengthening long. The back of her thighs pulled tight and the sensation of stretching grabbed her attention.

Relax.

She took a deeper breath, in and out, letting her muscles pull and stretch. *Just breathe and relax.*

After she sat up, she positioned her legs for *Ardha Matsyendrasana*, Half Spinal Twist Exercise. This asana was complicated and had taken Reba a long time to learn. She folded her left leg in, tucking the foot underneath her right hip. Then crossing her right foot over her left knee, she turned her upper body to the right, bracing her left elbow into her right knee. With the push of her arm against the knee, she twisted further and tighter, bringing her chin to her right shoulder. She felt her insides wringing out, the nice twisting sensation in her abdomen deepening. Then she untwisted herself, crossed her legs the opposite way and twisted to the left.

As she untwisted her spine, she felt the effects of her practice. Lying down on her back into final relaxation she closed her eyes, feeling energized but relaxed. Focused but calm. She would spend a few minutes in Shavasana, allowing her body to even out.[104]

It was all so simple in theory. No equipment, no machines, no contraptions. Just the correct asanas for each person. Just 5–6 a day. That is all it takes!

---

[104] Ibid.

Women had not always been allowed to practise yoga.[105] Reba was part of a new world where it was permitted and even encouraged. Traditional texts on yoga were always written from a male perspective; there is next to no evidence of women practising physical yoga to any significant extent prior to modernity. Throughout the history of yoga, little mention was made of women except when presenting them as a hindrance to the practice. A handful of Hatha Yoga texts from the fifteenth to the eighteenth centuries, including the well-known *Hatha Yoga Pradipika*, suggest that women should be avoided—along with cows, roads, dancing, wealth, etc.—if men are to have success in yoga.

Even Ramakrishna Paramahamsa spoke about women as an obstacle to the progress of yoga and warned of the dangers of women practising it. 'Be careful, householders!' he said. 'Put not too much confidence in women! They establish their mastery over you so very insidiously!'[106] Ramakrishna echoed the Hatha Yoga texts suggesting that women would prevent the accomplishment of yoga, stealing the attention of a seeker of God.[107] 'World-bound souls cannot resist the temptation of woman and wealth and direct their minds to God, even though these things bring upon them a thousand humiliations.'[108]

But a few short decades after Ramakrishna, his disciple Swami Vivekananda had a perspective that was more in line with the cultural reform movements of the time. Vivekananda echoed his contemporaries, 'The uplift of the women, the

---

[105] Mallinson and Singleton, *Roots of Yoga*, 53.
[106] Ramakrishna, *Teachings of Sri Ramakrishna* (Kolkata: Advaita Ashrama, 2012), 111, verse 300.
[107] Pajunen, 'Yoga in Bengal'.
[108] Ramakrishna, *Teachings of Sri Ramakrishna*, 110-1, Verse 299.

awakening of the masses must come first,' he said, 'then only can any real good come about for the country, for India.'[109] Put succinctly, 'The best thermometer to the progress of a nation is its treatment of women.'[110]

Here too, yoga was evolving in complex ways. Vivekananda taught the four paths of yogas—*karma, bhakti, raja, jnana*—none of which were Hatha Yoga. Vivekananda reshaped the history of yoga, beliefs and practices and translated them into ideas accessible for his times.[111] The four yogas were meant to be an accessible way to learn and teach Vedanta, the 'universal religion' that could accommodate all religious needs and systems through yoga.[112] But as yoga continued to evolve and reshape itself to fit in the world, more and more emphasis was placed on asanas and pranayama. Vivekananda's ideals blended in with the physical cultures being practised in the akharas. The circus, magic and stage acts incorporated the mysticism of spiritual practices, but for the sake of performance. All of this influenced yoga.

The 'women's issue' had plagued Indian society for decades. Societal trends were unsure how to modernize some traditions regarding women and their education which were portrayed by the British as uncivilized. Male reform leaders in India spoke out to change or abandon customs such as purdah and the practice of sati. Sati in particular was considered by the British to be quite barbaric. Such practices were a means to justify colonial

---

[109] Vivekananda, *Teachings of Swami Vivekananda* (Kolkata: Advaita Ashrama, 2014), 133.
[110] Ibid., 125.
[111] Elizabeth De Michelis. *A History of Modern Yoga* (London: Continuum, 2004), 3.
[112] Ibid., 123.

dominance because these gave Westerners an opportunity to paint Indian culture as outdated, brutal and backward. So the colonized culture in India shifted in some ways by updating the view of women, adjusting how they were treated in society and expanding the opportunities that were open to them.

But not all the opportunities that wealthy and socially progressive modern Western women had—like education, a freer choice of clothing and hiring domestic help—were attractive to Bengali women. To many, the highest form of femininity was to be a wife or mother. Some thought that Westernization could lead towards promiscuity or laziness in women. For them, the ideal feminine roles were keeping a house and cooking. As Western women began hiring out these jobs to allow for their own leisure time, maids and servants did the majority of the housework. Many Bengalis frowned upon this, as they thought it led to poor housekeeping. A hired worker would never do as good a job as the woman of the house. Furthermore, the family secrets passed down through generations from mother to daughter would be lost if they stopped caring for the food and home. Without the women carrying on the traditional roles of family, the fear was that family itself would fall apart.

Even Ghosh himself warned against the dangers of women's emancipation if done without care. 'My dear ladies,' he wrote, 'the unrestrained manner in which you dress and behave in public is not a sign of progress or development, as you wrongfully claim! Rather, it is stark evidence of lost self-control and discipline in your minds and character.'[113] He emphasized that the ideal role of a

---

[113] Bishnu Charan Ghosh, 'Bengal Women Beware', *Byayam Charcha*. Exact issue unknown.

woman was as a mother, holding together not only the family but also the whole of society.

'Great men were born of Bengali women', he wrote, giving examples of the women who birthed great sages and leaders of Bengal like Ramakrishna, Vivekananda and Aurobindo. He warned, 'If you cannot follow their ideals, you cannot give birth to such great sons—Bengal is drowning in all spheres and you are its saviour.'[114]

In the years before Reba began studying at Ghosh's college, women were getting involved in physical education and education at large. But they often felt that physical conditioning would make them less feminine or damage them in some way; or achieving physical strength was impossible for them altogether. So the movement to strengthen India's women emphasized the woman's role at home, highlighting how physical fitness can make her a better *wife* and *mother*. It also had to be done in a way that stressed upon the traditional values of modesty and purity. Vivekananda warned that any development of women's intellect should not be done at the cost of purity.[115] This was not so much an issue with a practice like yoga, which was often associated with increased purity. The *Gheranda Samhita*, a yoga text from the late seventeenth century states, 'Like an unbaked pot in water, the body is always decaying. One should bake it with the fire of Yoga and make it *pure*.'[116]

However, this fear of losing tradition could not outweigh the pressing issue of female oppression. The 'new woman' was

---

[114] Ibid.
[115] Vivekananda, *Teachings of Swami Vivekananda*, 130.
[116] *Gheranda Samhita*, 1.8., Trans. James Mallinson (YogaVidya.com. Woodstock, NY: YogaVidya.com, 2004), 3.

on her way, even if her existence was defined through her relationship with men.[117] The world of men was the external world, the world of work, strength, trade, money and war. This world had been colonized, dominated by the Western oppressors. But the world of women was internal, the realm of the home, family, tradition, ritual, religion and spirituality, at least metaphorically.

This was more private and protected from the outside forces. At home, in the internal world of the Indian woman, Indian society was always free. This was the realm of the female. Thus, women became the carriers of the true Indian identity.[118]

A great rewriting of women in Indian society was under way, and Reba's growing knowledge of yoga was one small part of it.

After her asana practice Reba would practise pranayama, the breath control of yoga.

'Come, Reba!' Byayamacharya Ghosh's voice commanded her out of Shavasana. 'I will teach you pranayam!'

With that, she moved from the physical to the more subtle and even mystical realm of the breath.

Ghosh started by teaching her *Sitali Pranayam*.[119]

'*Ekhane eshe bosho* (come and sit here),' he instructed, pointing to the ground in front of him. 'Cross your legs. Sit up straight.'

Reba sat, legs folded, backbone straight, body flexible. She looked at her guru, waiting for his next instruction.

---

[117] Partha Chatterjee, *The Nation and Its Fragments: Colonial and Postcolonial Histories* (Princeton: Princeton University Press, 1994), 127.
[118] Ibid.
[119] Rakshit, 'The Sport of Elephant Lifting', 253-64.

'Now usually we breathe through the nose,' he said. 'This pranayam must be done through the throat. *Ahhh* at the time of inhaling and *khi* at the time of exhaling by constricting the vocal cords.'

Reba tried to do as he said, breathing through her throat and making a small sound.[120]

Byayamacharya Ghosh counted.

'Inhale. One, two, three, four…'

She kept inhaling, careful to make her breath smooth, not halting it, and making a rattling noise as the count crept higher.

'Six, seven, eight.'

Her lungs were full!

I hope he doesn't keep counting higher! she thought.

'Exhale,' he said. 'One, two, three, four … '

Reba slowly emptied her lungs, making a 'khi' sound in her throat. After several long breaths in this manner, Reba was calm and focused, in a strange state that was not like anything else in this world. There was a buzzing in her ears.

Then came the second part.

Ghosh told her, 'Now roll your tongue. Breathe in through the rolled tongue and exhale through the nose, making the same sounds! This is Sitali Pranayam.'

He explained the benefits. *Sitali* means 'she who is cool'; so it was thought to cool the body and destroy toxins. Centuries before, sitali was taught as a means to deal with an inflamed spleen and to reduce fever.[121] Ghosh said that Sitali Pranayam would make for better pulmonary opening, make

---

[120] These instructions are taken from P.S. Das, *Yoga Panacea* (Kolkata: Indian Publishing House, 2004), 192.

[121] Mallinson and Singleton, *Roots of Yoga*, 158.

her breathing more efficient and make her able to control diseases.

And most importantly, he said, 'Pranayam will enhance your strength so much that you will remain unscathed even if an elephant walks over you.'[122]

Reba stopped breathing for a moment.

What? An elephant! This is probably an exaggeration, she thought, though she could not be sure because something about his tone made her think that he was being serious. She continued the breathing practice, trying not to think too much about it. *An elephant ... no.*

But Ghosh continued, 'Once you master the Sitali Pranayam, a motorcyclist will ride over you at full speed!'

A motorcycle! Reba's ears were perked now. She lost all focus on her breathing. She took some comfort knowing that an elephant was not easily acquired outside of the circus, but she knew that the Ghosh family had motorcycles.

Maybe he is serious.

Then it became clear. *He was serious.*

'Don't fret,' he said, 'nothing will happen to you.'[123]

---

[122] Rakshit, 'The Sport of Elephant Lifting', 253-264.
[123] Ibid.

11

Passing the Test with Flying Colours

How Reba Mastered Her Breath Control

Ghosh and Reba were becoming a team. Although their relationship was complicated, as most are, he represented her, and she began to be an important representative of Ghosh's college. To the world, he was a powerful byayamacharya. To a select few, he was their guru. To Reba, he was both of those things. And as time together strengthened their relationship, Reba affectionately started calling him Bishtuda.

Ghosh loved motorcycles. Something powerful overcame him when he straddled the leather seat and rested his hands upon the handlebars of a motorcycle. When he squeezed the clutch and revved up the engine, he felt the power of the machine growling underneath him, so loud that it drowned out any voices or sounds of the world around him. He simply could not control himself. He wanted to disappear into the roar of the engine with the sting of the wind on his face.

He wanted to drive fast.

When he described the sensation of motorcycle riding, he said, 'It would fill the entire length of the Mahabharata to talk about all the thrilling and spine-chilling experiences.'[124]

And if anyone tried to race him, he would ensure that they lost.

He always wanted to win.

He would make sure his victory was so significant that a witness would have enough time to take a large drink out of a fresh coconut between his glorious finish and when the loser whizzed past. But even winning was not enough. Given his boyish, impish nature, he would even taunt the loser. He made fun of their riding style and berated them for their poor finish.

Sometimes Ghosh zoomed down the streets of Calcutta, weaving in between cars and pedestrians at high speed. One day, he sped past the police chief, Mr Colson, on his BMW motorcycle. His speed was so alarming that Colson stopped him the next day with a warning.

'Not only is it dangerous for everyone else,' Colson scolded, 'but you are putting yourself in danger. If you crashed, you would be seriously injured or killed.'

'God always looks after me and saves me,' Ghosh replied with a smile.

But Colson was not about to back down.

---

[124] Bishnu Charan Ghosh, 'Towards the Past', *Byayam Charcha*, April (1966).

'God may be absent-minded one day.'[125]

One of Ghosh's students, Pravas Bandopadhyaya, was also crazy about motorcycles. He was the byayam teacher at a school near Golf Green. The Behala Motorbike Race[126] was a popular competition held in a short distance away. This was no ordinary race. The competition had a singular twist—every bike required two riders and a potato. The potato was placed between the two, pushed against the back of the rider's head and held in place by the forehead of the person riding pillion. They could not use their hands or any other instrument, only the pressing of the two heads could hold the potato. To win, the potato had to stay in place for the entirety of the race. It could not drop, even as the bike bounced up and down across the uneven ground. Pravas invited Ghosh to the event as a spectator. Ghosh simply could not resist, so he took his promising young student Reba along. However, as the whistle was about to be blown to start the race, Pravas cried out, 'Wait, wait! Guruji, you *must* participate!'

Reba agreed enthusiastically.

'Come, Bishtuda! Let's enter the race!'

The challenge kindled her adventurous nature.

That day she had come dressed in salwar kameez. She wasted no time in kicking off her slippers and jumping on the back of her Bishtuda's bike. The seat on the back of the bike was small, perched right above the rear wheel on its fender.

---

[125] Ibid.
[126] This happened in 1953.

She tied her brightly coloured dupatta tightly and tucked it around her waist.

When the whistle blew, they tore off, Reba's forehead pressed firmly into the potato.

The power of the motorcycle's acceleration combined with the unusual balance of the potato threw many inexperienced riders into the air. Some tumbled off the back of their bikes, some lost their balance and had to slow down. Everywhere potatoes were dropping, one by one.

Ghosh started off in second gear, accelerating slowly being careful not to be thrown off suddenly on the unfamiliar road. After a few moments, the pair got a feel for the bumps in the street.

Ghosh yelled as loud as he could, '*Reba*! Grip my neck hard!'[127]

She wrapped her hands around his neck, careful not to cover his eyes. She pulled his head towards her, pinning the potato between them. They reached full speed, flying across the course with only one other competitor nearby. The rutted ground was no match for their precision, balance and strength. Ghosh focused intently on the road, steering the bike while Reba kept her attention on keeping the potato in place. They both laughed, the roar of the engine rang in their ears and the smell of the city wind wafted through their noses.

They pulled away from their last competitor and crossed the finish line with no one in sight.

The small crowd that was gathered at the finish line cheered as Ghosh and Reba got down from their bike, smiling. Their potato finally fell to the ground. Reba had a large red mark on her forehead from where the potato had been pressing.

---

[127] Ghosh, 'Towards the Past'.

She touched it with her fingers, laughing, as the race official approached to give their award.

'Unseating the reigning champ, Mr Jack Willis,' the announcer began,[128] 'the new winner is the only Bengali to enter the race! Sri Bishnuuu Charaaan Ghooooshhhh!'

His voice boomed down the avenue. The crowd cheered as the announcer continued, 'The winner is Bishnu Ghosh, but today the prize must be given to Reba Rakshit!'

Everyone waited for an explanation.

'If it was not for her, he would have never entered the race!'

Ghosh and Reba happily rode back to north Calcutta that afternoon with Reba proudly holding the trophy in her hand.

After school one day, Reba made her way to Ghosh's college. As she walked through the gates of the college, Ghosh came down the stairs. It was odd for him to come outside to meet her because they usually met in his office or in one of the practice rooms. When he reached the bottom of the stairs, he passed underneath the giant tree in the courtyard and headed towards the motorcycle parked outside the gate.

'Come, Reba,' he said. 'Today is the day you take your pranayam exam. You must pass!'[129]

Reba did not mind because she was a good student. And she hoped that if she passed, she would be initiated into even more powerful yogic practices. She nodded and looked at him, eagerly waiting for his instructions.

---

[128] Ibid.
[129] Rakshit, 'The Sport of Elephant Lifting', 253-264.

Pranayama was a primary physical practice of yoga prior to the modern age.[130] Combining the word for 'lifebreath (*prana*)' with 'control (*ayama*)', two paths of practice developed.[131] One path used pranayama for mystical ends while the other was a part of ascetic practice.[132]

In some of the ancient texts of India—as in the Dharmasastras that explain law and conduct—pranayama is viewed as penance.[133] Controlling the breath has the ability to cleanse or remove bad karma.

Much later, in the handful of centuries leading up to the day when Reba entered Ghosh's college, pranayama had a new interpretation. *Hatha* means 'force', so Hatha Yoga was the yoga of force.[134] It consisted of manipulating the body by means of mudras or seals, turning it upside down to shift the direction of energy with *viparita karani*, or controlling the breath with pranayama. As Hatha Yoga expanded to include a larger number of practices including asanas, ideas arose that the practice of pranayama could bring about supernatural powers. Some texts suggested that it could awaken the serpent goddess energy kundalini;[135] others taught that the practices were directly linked to liberation.

---

[130] Mallinson and Singleton, *Roots of Yoga*, 127.

[131] It is a common misunderstanding that the word pranayama is a combination of the words *prana* and *yama* or *prāna* and *ayama*. In truth, it combines the words *prana* and *āyāma*, meaning 'control'. So *pranayama* is control of *prana*. Mallinson and Singleton, *Roots of Yoga*, 128.

[132] Ibid.

[133] Law Code of Manu, 6.69–70, *The Law Code of Manu*, trans. Patrick Olivelle (Oxford: Oxford University Press, 2004), 103.

[134] Jason Birch, 'The Meaning of *Hatha* in Early Hathayoga', *Journal of the American Oriental Society*, 131.4, 527–54.

[135] Mallinson and Singleton, *Roots of Yoga*, 133.

Texts also gave warnings about the pain, difficulty and the dangerous ramifications of lengthening or stopping the breath. The practice was often equated with asceticism and the idea that through painful practice karma could be eliminated and rebirth avoided. Somewhere in the tenth to eleventh centuries, the idea surfaced that breath control would surely harm the body. Even the later Hatha Yoga texts suggested that, though beneficial, pranayama could be dangerous.[136] The *Hatha Yoga Pradipika* issued a warning: 'Just as a lion, elephant, or tiger is tamed step by step, so the breath is controlled. Otherwise, it kills the practitioner.'[137] One commentary even suggested that excessive practice could lead to abdominal problems as well as insanity.[138]

Elsewhere, controlling the breath could create a link between life, the breath and the mind. When Kalidasa, strived to capture an image of Lord Shiva in meditation, he wrote about the profound stillness that comes through controlling the breath.

> As a result of restraining his inner winds
> He was like a cloud without a rage of rain,
> Like a pot of water without a ripple,
> Like a flickering lamp in a place without wind.[139]

---

[136] This was taught by the Shaiva scholar Abhinavagupta. Mallinson and Singleton, *Roots of Yoga*, 127–28.

[137] *Hatha Yoga Pradipika*, 2.15, *The Hatha Yoga Pradipika* trans. Brian Dana Akers (YogaVidya.com, Woodstock, NY, 2002), 36.

[138] From a commentary on the *Mrgendratantra*. Mallinson and Singleton, *Roots of Yoga*, 37–38, 128.

[139] *Kumarasambhavam*, 3.44–50. Mallinson and Singleton, *Roots of Yoga*, 143.

Controlling the breath is a way to control the mind. When the breath is moving, the mind also moves. To make the mind calm and still, control of the breath has to be mastered. As the *Chandogya Upanishad*, one of India's oldest sacred texts, states:

> Just as a bird tied by a string flies off in all directions and, on not reaching any other place to stay, returns to where it is tied, in the very same way, dear boy, the mind flies off in all directions and, on not reaching any other place to stay, returns to the breath. For the mind, dear boy, is tied to the breath.[140]

Reba learned to control her breath under the guidance of her guru.

'This is what you must do,' Ghosh said. 'Inhale a little bit of air, and then *stop* the exhaling for a few moments.'

Reba listened intently. It did not sound exactly like the other pranayamas she had learned, but thought it must be part of the exam.

He continued, 'You don't need to bother doing anything else. Be careful. Don't release the air from your lungs.'[141]

By this time Reba was comfortable controlling her breath, and holding it did not seem difficult. Even as a little girl when she was swimming in the lakes near her home in Comilla she had practised holding her breath, timing each inhale precisely for the moment that her face was out of the water. *This exam doesn't seem too hard*, she thought. The only possible problem was if he asked her to hold her breath for a very long time,

---

[140] *Chandogya Upanishad* 6.8.2. Mallinson and Singleton, *Roots of Yoga*, 138.
[141] Rakshit, 'The Sport of Elephant Lifting', 253-264.

more than two or three minutes. *How long must I hold my breath?* she wondered.

Then, as Ghosh gave the next instruction, her heart sank.

'You will naturally feel when the motorcycle has passed over your body. Release the air then.'[142]

Reba was shocked.

And confused.

A motorcycle will pass over my body! That sounds a lot like being run over. She knew that some of Ghosh's male students would lift heavy things on their chests, but she could never imagine that he would ask her to do it.

She took a moment to take it all in, and then she pleaded with Ghosh. 'Oh My God! No, *No*! I cannot do this! I will *die*!'[143]

Ghosh was firm. 'Nothing will happen! *Thik parbi*! You can do it!'

He was convinced that Reba was ready for the stunt. If he had any worries about her safety, he did not reveal them then.

Reba's heart started beating frantically; blood rushed to her face and she suddenly felt very hot. She looked right and left, as if looking for a way out.

'Nothing will happen! You can do it!' he repeated confidently. His own determination and willpower were convincing. Gradually Reba began to calm down, soothed by Bishtuda's confidence and her own slow breathing. Whatever concerns for personal safety or well-being that could have got in the way were overpowered by his steady conviction.

---

[142] Ibid.
[143] Ibid.

He has done this before. I'm sure he knows what he's doing, she thought. Also, Reba was determined not to displease her guru.[144]

'You lie down and I'll place a strong plank over you.'

Ghosh was setting up the stunt as Reba listened blankly.

'A motorcyclist will run over you at full speed. Don't fret, nothing will happen to you.'[145]

Lifting motorcycles is not so much about the weight. The bike approaches quickly, skips over most of the body and is airborne for much of the stunt. The stunt is very fast. Before you realize it has begun, it has long since finished.

The difficulty of lifting the motorcycle is withstanding the force of it hitting your side before flying up into the air. Imagine the force of steel having accelerated to full speed before it hits your ribs like a speed bump. It is this jerking motion that is dangerous. There is only one thing that can prevent your ribs from cracking like sticks on impact. That is a tiny pocket of air, carefully being held in the lungs with as much care, tenderness and control as possible.

Reba accepted what she was about to do.

She stopped thinking and made her mind quiet.

She did what her guru asked.

She walked towards the wooden plank and lay down in the middle of the alleyway, her head towards one side of the road and her feet towards the other. Ghosh lifted the end of the plank and placed it across her chest. It was thick, about two hands wide and the length of two tall men. Reba braced herself as the weight of the plank settled on top of her.

---

[144] Ibid.
[145] Ibid.

Ghosh finished arranging the plank, stood up and stepped back. He gave Reba his final instructions.

'Immediately hold your breath the moment I shout "breathe" and exhale when the bike has passed.'[146]

Reba's heart was thumping with so much force she thought perhaps the wooden plank would bounce up and down with each beat.

Ghosh said, 'I promise you won't even feel it.'[147]

She heard the motorcycle's engine roar in the distance, down the alley to her right, but she could not even turn her head to see. She heard it approaching quickly.

It was then that Reba's senses went dormant. All the world became silent; she only listened intently for Ghosh's instruction to breathe. He was standing a few feet away from her, above her head, leaning in slightly and watching closely as the stunt unfolded. When she heard her guru shout '*Breathe!*' she quickly inhaled a little and held her breath. Her mind stopped and it seemed that the world had stopped too. As the motorcycle passed over her, she felt a small amount of pressure on her chest, but her breath was strong, almost as if she could throw the weightless little machine into the air with the yogic power of her breath. In an instant, the bike passed over her. The weight disappeared from her chest just as quickly as it had come.

It was done.

She exhaled.

As Ghosh came towards her and removed the plank from her chest, Reba was immediately overwhelmed by two *very*

---

[146] Ibid.
[147] Ibid.

opposite feelings. One was of relief that she had survived intact.

I am still alive!

And the other was a deeper sense that this was only the beginning of her power. If she could lift a motorcycle with such ease, what else could she do? Her mind whirled with possibilities. These two feelings seemed to cancel each other out and she felt numb. Nothing at all. No fear. No anxiety. No excitement. As if the motorcycle had picked up her emotions as it passed over her, pulled them from inside of her and carried them away down the street as it went.

She could not understand what had happened. She could not *feel*.[148]

Perhaps she had transcended the body, passing her pranayama exam. Or perhaps her teenage body was in a state of shock leaving her numb.

Reba simply could not comprehend what had happened. It was too much to process in the moment.

But Ghosh had come to two very important conclusions of his own that day. The first was that Reba had successfully completed the trick. She passed the exam. She had taken to his training with great precision. She knew the asanas. She had mastered pranayama. He was confident that she could handle a life-or-death stunt.

And the second conclusion was that Reba was capable of more.

---

[148] Ibid.

12

Reba the Star Is Born

The World Had Never Seen Anyone Like Her Before

Reba's success in the motorcycle stunt marked a turning point in her life. Thereafter, she began to seriously develop her physical strength. She continued going to Ghosh's college daily after her studies, training her body to be flexible and powerful, and her mind to be determined and courageous. Her training was no longer restricted to asanas and pranayama. She was also becoming strong—very strong. This meant taking up weight training, which was unique for a young woman in those days.

Ghosh was also an authority on bodybuilding and weightlifting; the ground floor of his school was dedicated to feats of strength and the practice of muscle control. A few of his star students like Buddha Bose excelled in asanas, but most of them were incredible physical culturists who focused on bodybuilding and performative feats of strength. Reba too began training just like the men.

Ghosh insisted that anyone could learn muscle building and control if they did it with care. He had seen the effects it had on people, including his own nephew Bijoy Kumar Mallick. As a boy, doctors told Bijoy that he would not mature well or even be able to read. But he took up muscle building at the age of sixteen and grew into a strong and powerful man.

'When you find time to sleep, to take your bath, to take your meals,' Ghosh said often, 'you can easily find time for a little exercise which is no less important than any other dire necessity of life.'[149]

For him and his students, maintaining health and gaining strength were a way of life.

Ghosh explained the next steps to Reba.

'You have become strong and flexible from your yoga asanas. And you have learned to control your breath, which gives you great power. Now you will develop your muscles and then you will learn muscle control.'

'What is muscle control?'

'Muscle control is the ability to contract certain muscles at will while all the others are relaxed.'

'But why can't I do that now?'

'No. First you must build your strength, your muscles. Muscle control is only impressive and noteworthy if there is some muscle mass there to see.'

'Why is it important to look impressive?'

'We must give our attention to what will be impressive onstage.'

---

[149] Bishnu Charan Ghosh and Keshub Ch. Sen Gupta, *Muscle Control and Barbell Exercise* (Calcutta: Published by the authors, 1930), 51.

Reba had shown promise in the motorcycle stunt. She had proved to her guru that she was brave and curious. Ghosh was preparing her to become a performer.

'*Thik achhe* (okay),' Reba said.

It is similar to pranayama practices, she thought. *First you learn to control the breath and make the sound. Then later you hold the breath and it gives you great power.*

Initially she spent some time training for health like everyone else, but now she was also training for *show*. This meant that she would learn impressive movements like pressing a barbell. She would lift the long thin metal rod with weights on each end all the way up and over her head, like she had seen the men do on her first visit to the college. Once the weight was overhead, she had to maintain perfect balance underneath it. She had to practise staying composed under pressure, controlling her breath under the intense weight.

The hardest part of the barbell press was straightening her arms and lifting the weight straight overhead. So Reba practised religiously. To start, she placed the barbell up on top of two stools, one stool under each end. This brought the weight off the ground, so she did not have to start with it at her feet every time. She bent underneath the resting bar, positioning it behind her neck, high on her back, gripping it tightly and holding it at shoulder level. Then she stood up as straight as possible, lifting the barbell off the stools, legs a little apart, holding the weight on her shoulders. Very slowly she pushed the barbell from her shoulders up into the air, straightening her arms.

The muscles of her shoulders and arms burned, as though screaming in effort.

Her whole body braced against the weight; her feet and legs, her spine and abdomen. It was hard to breathe as she held the weight up. The effort used all her energy and focus.

Once the weight was all the way overhead, she lowered the bar slowly, carefully, back onto her shoulders. It rested there briefly. Then she pressed it up again, repeating the exercise ten times. This was the way to build strength, she was learning. *Triceps, deltoid and back. Triceps, deltoid and back*, she repeated to herself, drilling the names of the muscles into her memory.[150] These were the muscles working in this exercise. It was important to pay attention to them and know exactly what the exercise was for. If she was careless or distracted, she would only build ordinary, average strength. But if she wanted to build super strength, it required paying close attention to the way in which she was doing the exercises.

Reba also had to adjust her diet and sleep, making sure she was supplying her body with the energy and rest it needed. She needed to sleep at least seven hours; that is what was prescribed for muscle development. Also she had to eat simple food, to conscientiously follow the maxim 'eat to live, not live to eat'.[151]

'Don't eat too much,' Ghosh used to tell her often. He was greatly influenced by the yogic ideas of diet. Just as it says in the *Hatha Yoga Pradipika*, Ghosh instructed, 'It is important to keep the stomach one-quarter empty.'[152] This was difficult sometimes when she was famished or tired from her day's

---

[150] Ibid., Barbell Exercises Figure 2b.
[151] Ibid., Barbell Exercise General Instructions.
[152] *Hatha Yoga Pradipika*, 1.58. 'A moderate diet means eating satisfying, sweet food for Shiva's pleasure, while leaving the stomach one-quarter empty.' *The Hatha Yoga Pradpika*, trans. Brian Dana Akers. See also, Ghosh and Sen Gupta, *Muscle Control and Barbell Exercise*. Barbell Exercise General Instructions.

study and training. It was not only important to chew the food properly, but also feel each morsel of food which was providing vitality, strength and energy.[153] Lastly, it was important to enjoy each meal. Everything had to be done properly. That was the only way for perfect development and superhuman strength.

One day, as Reba was finishing her barbell presses, Ghosh came into the gym with a surprising news.

'Reba, you are performing onstage tomorrow.'

'Tomorrow! What do you mean?'

She was obviously stunned.

'*Chandannagare jabo* (We are going to Chandannagar). You are performing in the show.'

With that, he walked off.

Although Reba stood in silence, there was a slight stirring in her stomach and her heart was racing. She was caught somewhere between surprise, excitement and terror.

Tomorrow!

But for now, she went back to weightlifting. After all, she had to finish her practice.

The next morning when she arrived at Ghosh's college, she noticed a small bus waiting in the alley. Ghosh had hired it to take the troupe to Chandannagar, forty kilometres upriver from Calcutta, about two hours by car or bus. As Reba walked through the gate, Ghosh informed her that she would be performing the simple asanas only, no weights or stunts.

That is a relief.

She was good at asanas and superbly confident about their execution, but extremely nervous about giving a public performance.

---

[153] Ghosh and Sen Gupta, *Muscle Control and Barbell Exercise*.

As the bus crawled north towards Chandannagar on the weaving road alongside the Hooghly River, the clamouring of the city faded into the distance. The haze of the Calcutta sky cleared into a lovely glow of pink in the late morning sun. As the bus twisted and turned around each bend, gliding between trees which seemed to grow taller as they passed by, Reba was anxious and excited; and tried hard to stay calm by steadying her breath, making it rhythmic and smooth.

An hour or so had passed. It felt like time was ticking by slowly, but as they got closer Reba felt as though perhaps time would just stop altogether. She sat up taller. They had arrived, it was time to work.

Now they were performers, and Ghosh did not miss a beat. He called out at the top of his voice to anyone who could hear that there would be a show which simply should not be missed.

'Bodybuilders show! Come! Come!' he shouted, his booming voice rippling far and wide through the air.

The institute there had contracted Ghosh to provide consultation on their physical training programme and arranged for him to present a few shows. That day's show was bodybuilding. The stage was a simple raised platform on the side of the street. Reba sat to the side, watching as the crowd gathered.

When it was time for the performance to begin, Ghosh addressed the crowd. 'When you find time to sleep, to take your bath, to take your meals, you can easily find time for a little exercise which is no less important than any other necessity of life!'

Reba knew these words well but they were new to the audience, which was wide-eyed with curiosity and excitement, nodding their heads in agreement. Ghosh continued, 'Muscle controlling makes the muscles shapely and increases the power of application of strength! Let's begin the show!'[154]

One of the students from the college, a muscular and attractive young man, ascended the steps onto the stage and walked to the middle of the platform. He wore only a small pair of tight shorts with a leopard print. His legs, chest and arms were bare, showing off his impressive physique.

'Biceps! Contract,' called out Ghosh from the side of the stage.

The audience fixed their eyes on the lad, who clenched his left fist firmly, bending the arm from the elbow. Carefully, he focused his attention, looking almost meditative. This was a sign of Ghosh's training. It was not just physical, it was also the willpower required to do the exercises correctly. A calm, focused look came over his face as a huge lump of muscle protruded from his arm, rising between his elbow and shoulder. An audible *'ooh'* arose from the audience.

'Relax! Relax. Now, triceps! Contract!' Ghosh barked out an order.

The young man straightened his arm, causing his biceps to relax. Then he pushed his shoulder up towards his ear and moved his arm out and away from his chest. He grabbed his left wrist with his other hand and pulled. He kept his arm straight, causing the muscle on the back of his arm to contract, bulging like an upside down V below his shoulder.

As the audience gasped and admired, Ghosh explained.

'See,' he said loudly, 'controlling in this position. He can contract and relax, making it dance at his will!'

---

[154] Ghosh and Sen Gupta, *Muscle Control and Barbell Exercise*, 52.

The show carried on like this. As Ghosh called out the muscles one by one, the young man showed the muscle isolation on his own body. It was nothing new to Reba, she had seen many others practising the same at Ghosh's college. Every so often, Reba could sense Ghosh scanning the crowd for anyone who could be a good recruit for his school.

'Thigh! Right leg! Left leg! Then both legs!' The young man's muscles contracted one by one, making his body bounce and ripple.

Once the bodybuilding part of the show had concluded it was Reba's turn. Her legs felt shaky as she walked towards the stage. It was as if each step towards being the centre of attention caused her nerves to take over. She climbed up the handful of steps on the side of the stage. When she reached the top, she steadied herself and took one deep breath.

Inhale. Exhale.

Then she walked to the centre of the platform. She wore a white leotard with white tights, so her whole body was covered in tight, thin fabric. The audience could see every action of her limbs as she moved. She had to look down at her own feet, afraid to lift her eyes towards the crowd who stared at her with great anticipation. The attention of the sea of strangers was resting on her, waiting for her to do something remarkable.

To *be* remarkable.

It was suffocating; but it was also very exciting.

How often had she felt this type of attention? Never. She was just a young girl, yet an audience of all ages was watching *her*. As she stood pondering this, she could feel the nerves pulse through her body.

She stood frozen in the middle of the stage, her mind blank. Perhaps she would have stayed there forever if it were not for the clear call of her guru's voice.

'Next we present asana!' Ghosh announced in his booming voice.

Without skipping a beat, Reba began on cue, switching into autopilot. Her duty to perform suddenly wiped away all her fears. She was so well practised that the muscle memory took over. Her mind was fine-tuned. With focus and precision, she began her performance.

Reba demonstrated the asanas she had been learning. She balanced, twisted, bent her body into positions while Ghosh called out the benefits of each asana. As Reba performed a Standing Deep Breathing Exercise, something that looked very simple from the outside, Ghosh raved about the magical curing effects.

'Clears lungs, good for people with asthma and pulmonary diseases! Relaxes neck muscles! And ensures that the thyroid gland is working well!'[155]

As Reba twisted her spine, Ghosh explained in a commanding and confident tone, 'Good for back pain! Improves flexibility along the spine to all the limbs!'[156]

The crowd was enthusiastic about the performance despite the simple postures. They were captivated by the cure-all promise that the asana carried. Ghosh promised that anyone who came to learn yoga from him would get the chance to cure their aches and pains. He would prepare an individualized system tailored to their unique needs and conditions like age, height, weight. Be it constipation, dyspepsia, sluggish liver, high blood pressure, stunted

---

[155] This was taught to the author at Ghosh's college during a therapeutic yoga training in 2015.

[156] This was taught to the author at Ghosh's college during a therapeutic yoga training in 2015.

growth—Ghosh had a cure for all of these. That solution was through asanas and pranayama.

Obesity, for example, needed not only therapeutic exercises like Hand Stretching and Back and Front Kicking, but also required asana practice. Asanas like *Uttana Padasana* (Leg Lift Asana) or *Pavanamuktasana* (Wind Removing Asana) were especially tailored to help with this specific issue. Of course, it was impossible to say that one cure could work for everyone because age and other ailments were all factored in. What a sixty-year-old needed was not the same as what a fourteen-year-old did. Only Ghosh's special knowledge could select the proper regimen of exercises and asanas.

Reba's grace and precision along with Ghosh's convincing explanation left the crowd enthusiastic at the conclusion of the performance.

As entrepreneurship flourished with figures like Ghosh, the success of places like Ghosh's college hinged on performance. If no one saw what difference physical culture made to their health, it was impossible to build any support. Without clients, one could not earn a living. One could not convince anyone they wanted to be taught unless one could show them something remarkable.

Ghosh was happy when the performances were a success. More business would come to Ghosh's college when audience members joined and got their own therapeutic yoga prescriptions.

Something stirred in Reba when she heard the overwhelming applause at her performance. In the end, she was the one in plain view, whose every move was the centre of attention. Without her, there was no show. Perhaps someone else could take her place, but in this moment *she* was the show. It was her skill, her command of the stage, her will for perfection that made the moment possible. This was her first taste of success. Standing alone on the stage she felt her heart warm and swell. Now that she had felt it, she was not sure she would be able to live without it. The response from the audience not only made her feel appreciated, but it was also who she wanted to be. Getting past her nerves and through her first performance made her feel that anything was possible. Beyond that, she felt satisfaction with what she had done and a desire to press forward, to test herself, to test her ability, to test the appreciation of the audience.

At the end of her performance, Reba was uncertain how to act. She had seen performers who bowed and waved to their admiring fans, beaming confidently while standing in the middle of the stage. But she bowed awkwardly as the applause continued, unsure how to respond to the admiration from the audience. Then she turned and walked directly to the edge of the stage and down the stairs, past where Ghosh was standing. Her body and mind were humming. Slowly her nervous system relaxed and she felt her heart beat more slowly. But her body stiffened and began to ache. As the adrenaline eased from her muscles, she felt both tired and strained, a sort of performance hangover. She had felt soreness before, usually a day or two after exercising her body intensely. When she stretched deeply towards her toes in Paschimottanasana, she would get sore hamstrings on the back of her thighs. When she did many repetitions of *Bhujangasana* and Dhanurasana, her back muscles felt sore. Now that she was lifting weights, she would feel soreness in the muscles she exercised. Often her shoulders and arms were too sore to move the day after a hard session. But this achy feeling was new; it seemed to come from the let-down after the intense psychological high of performing onstage.

How far can I go with my performances? Just how far can I take myself? At that moment, it did not occur to her that she would ever stop. Although it was only her first performance, she was hooked. On seeing the audience positively respond to Reba's act, Ghosh said, 'Reba, we have two more performances this week. Be ready.'

Her guru was always clear in his vision, never second-guessing himself, not persuaded by doubt. As soon as Reba heard this, she silently informed the world: *Yes, get ready for Reba Rakshit! You've never seen anyone like her before.*

Reba settled into her new routine of school, training and performance. She gave performances two or three times a week, while adhering to a strict training routine. She was increasingly becoming busy. As Reba started spending more time at Ghosh's college or out of town for performance, Suhasini became worried about her daughter's future.

One afternoon, Suhasini went to the college to confront her daughter's guru. She walked up the steps to Ghosh's office. As she turned down the hallway, she caught Reba's gaze. Reba was in the women's room, practising her asanas. Suhasini paused, reaching to make sure the *anchal* of her saree was still pinned properly. Then she entered the square office.

'Please come in,' Ghosh said politely. '*Boshun* (sit).'

Suhasini gently closed the door behind her and sat in the big wooden chair in front of Ghosh's desk. The sounds of men and women counting, *1 ... 2 ... 3 ...*, could be heard faintly from outside.

'Sri Byayamacharya, I have come to speak to you about my daughter, Reba,' Suhasini said.

'Yes, go on.'

As soon as he spoke, the door opened and he motioned someone in. Suhasini turned in her chair. Someone had come with tea.

'*Cha khaben* (Will you drink some tea?)?' Ghosh asked.

'*Haan khabo* (yes).'

She took the small cup of tea in her hands, feeling the heat of the hot tea on her fingertips. She took a sip, lowered her cup and looked at Ghosh.

'My daughter cannot learn your yoga anymore,' she said. She was calm but direct.

'What will happen to her studies if this continues? She has no time to study, no time to learn anything else, no time for school. She is always practising, and now, even worse, running around to different cities to perform.'

After seeing her mother enter, Reba had crept down the hallway after her. She stealthily put her ear to the thick door to listen in. She wanted to keep learning yoga and was worried that her mother would stand in the way of her dream. As she waited to hear who would speak next, Ghosh spoke. 'How does this affect her study? She is learning yoga. That's all.'

Suhasini looked at him, but he did not wait for her to respond. 'She will go on learning yoga. She can learn for a few hours in the afternoon. That's all. Yoga and study go hand in hand. They are complementary. You cannot separate the two. Even my brother Swami Yogananda knows this to be true.'

It had been part of the mission of the two brothers for decades to develop a connection between school learning, physical health and spiritual development. Back in the 1930s, when Reba was a small girl in Comilla, the brothers had travelled all through India attempting to gain funding for such a venture that would revamp school curriculum around the country.

Before that, Yogananda had started a small school which moved several times. It began in the same north Calcutta neighbourhood, just a couple of blocks from Ghosh's college. In fact, Ghosh had been among the first batch of students. The school finally settled somewhere west in Ranchi, where it still was. Yogananda's facilities were expanding, turning into the spiritually focused Yogoda Satsanga hubs. Their efforts to win funding and support for educational institutions were unsuccessful in the end, and eventually the entire endeavour was overrun by World War II. Nevertheless, this mission to combine school with physical training was deeply Yogananda's bones.

'Learning yoga will not hinder Reba's school learning. On the contrary, it will facilitate it. Moreover, she will learn yoga in the afternoon,' Ghosh said.

With that, Reba scurried back down the hallway and into the women's yoga room.

Suhasini placed her empty teacup on the table and stood up. Her attempted intervention was clearly over, and there was no way to change what was already in motion. Reba was learning yoga. Suhasini could do nothing but pray it did not harm her daughter's future.

Stuntmaster Reba —a Class Act

13

'I Felt Nothing At All'

How Reba Felt When a Baby Elephant Walked over Her

Reba mastered the art of lifting motorcycles. Her pranayama was well-developed and she could control her breath to generate immense power. After a few months onstage, she had adapted well to the pressure of being the centre of attention. She remained absolutely calm in the spotlight. Sometimes, she even felt like she could control the audience's emotions just by concentrating her energy. She still got the aches and pains occasionally, which came after the performance and once the adrenaline had drained from her body. But she was slowly getting used to it. The aches mostly happened after big performances when she was more nervous than usual.

Her guru was always ready with something more for her. It was typical of him. Talent meant potential and potential meant more and bigger performance opportunities. A single ounce of success opened the door for greater accomplishments in the future. Hence, Ghosh was always brainstorming new ideas, new stunts and new performances.

The first time Reba heard about Ghosh's plan for her to lift an elephant was when he was brainstorming new ideas for their performances with a senior teacher at the college. They were standing in the courtyard while Reba was in the gym lifting weights.

'Let me see if she can do it or not!' Ghosh said excitedly.

'Has a woman ever lifted an elephant before?'

'I don't think so. We will not let that stop us. But there is always a first time.'

'I am not sure that it is safe for a woman.'

'It will make the stunt even more impressive if a thin, elegant woman like Reba performs it,' Ghosh said. 'She is a good student and good onstage. She is strong and concentrated. We can start with a baby elephant.'

Ghosh had clearly made up his mind. And once his mind was made up, there was no changing it.[157] His self-confidence and charisma made it difficult for anyone to oppose him.

Reba had performed so well with the motorcycle that crowds were already taking note of her beauty and her talent. Ghosh was fixated on the idea of Reba lifting an elephant.

When he finally broke the news to Reba, she just could not believe her ears.

An elephant! That's impossible.

She shook it off. But could not help thinking …

After all, it must be nearly impossible to find an elephant. It was not like there were elephants simply roaming the streets of

---

[157] Rakshit, 'The Sport of Elephant Lifting', 253-264.

Calcutta![158] Motorcycles, though somewhat rare, were much more common. When Ghosh craved the thrill of a motorcycle stunt, he simply requested Pravas to bring his motorbike and it was arranged almost immediately. But even Ghosh, with his strong will and vision, could not simply manifest an elephant in the middle of the crowded Calcutta streets, or could he? And even if the giant creature suddenly appeared in the courtyard of Ghosh's college, he could not just command, 'Walk on Reba's chest!' and expect it to obey. A wild elephant answered to no one, and even a trained elephant would only answer to the command of its personal mahout.

With all of those barriers comforting Reba, she rested easy. *It simply would not happen.*

Or so she thought.

While the classic Greek and Roman cultures depicted the horse far more than the elephant, in India the elephant has been central to fables, epic stories and scriptures. Nowhere was the relationship between humans and elephants more loving than in India. The elephant has been a sign of good luck, power and greatness since time immemorial. It has been part of myths, festivals and the Hindu religion, Lord Ganesha being one of the most popular deities.

It is believed that even Lord Buddha was an elephant in one of his previous lives. He was pearly white, with six massive tusks, and led a herd of 8,000 animals.

Elephants were about to become an intimate part of Reba's life. While elephant legends live *in* the hearts of those

---

[158] Ibid.

who hear them, for Reba the elephant itself would live *on* her heart, and the legend would be written in the space of one held breath at a time.

A circus company was visiting Calcutta. With scheduled performances in the afternoons and evenings, the mornings were free time for the acrobats, clowns and magicians, as well as the animals.

Ghosh managed to contact the circus owner with the following proposal:

'I have a highly skilled and beautiful young woman who is stronger than any you've ever seen. She has other-worldly yogic strength beyond that of even a man. I'd like to bring her to the circus in the morning.'

'A strong woman? I'm very interested,' replied the circus man. 'What does she lift?'

'She lifts weights, and she can lift a motorcycle on her chest with ease.'

'*Khubi bhalo* (very good). You can bring her here. Come in the morning.'

'When I bring her, I will need to use one of your elephants, a small one.'

'*Ashambhab* (impossible)! Only our handlers are allowed to ride the elephants.'

'Not for riding. She will lift it on her chest.'

Silence struck the conversation. Then, a decisive response came from the circus agent.

'That is impossible. She will be crushed like an ant, like a spider.'

'No that will not happen,' Ghosh insisted. 'I'm telling you, you have never seen a person this strong and powerful, let alone a woman.'

'Okay, I'd like to see her try. If she dies, neither I nor the circus should be held responsible.'

'She will not die. You will see.'

'Very well. Bring her in the morning. We have a young elephant you can use, one-year-old.'

What may have been an unexpected and absurd conversation to most was just another day in the circus. After all, it was a commonly held belief that the circus animals were just taking up space and eating up profit anytime they were not in the ring performing for the audience. Free time was perfect to try new tricks— something more impossible, more impressive, more spectacular.

A young, thin, beautiful girl taking an elephant on her chest? Ghosh had spun the request to be irresistible.

When Reba informed her family about her Bishtuda's plan, not a single one of them thought it was a good idea. Her parents were completely horrified and dismayed and her brothers were adamant that she should not go.

However, Ghosh prodded Jyotsna when she came to the college to pick up Reba.

'Come and see for yourself! She will take an elephant on her chest! Come! Come!'

But Jyotsna did not dare.

'I will most certainly not come along! And furthermore, I will not listen to this crazy idea. You're going to get her killed!'[159]

---

[159] Ibid.

Already Reba's performances were a tense subject with her family. She had just finished her matriculation examinations in school. They thought she needed to focus more on her studies and build her future, and not chase some silly dream of stardom. And now she was adding fatal danger to the conversation at home. The family members thought it was a terrible, unthinkable idea, they all agreed.

But Reba had to go. She would not ignore her Bishtuda's request, no matter what it was. He was her guru. She trusted him more than herself, more than even her parents. If he said it was what she should do, she would do it. So, the duo went to the circus early one morning.

As they approached the circus grounds, she could see elephants standing in the field beyond the main tent. The massive creatures seemed so alien, so slow.

Their presence was simply incomprehensible to her. How could a creature be so commanding, yet appear so gentle and calm? As Reba and Ghosh walked across the grass field towards the animals, her sandals sank into the soft earth, still cool and moist from the night. The smell of animal feed, hay and dung grew stronger as they approached.

Thud, clank! Thud, clank, clank! In the distance, she heard a metallic sound ring out, cutting through the quiet morning.

She looked around for the source of the sound, but the rest of the circus was empty and silent this morning. It seemed to be coming from the elephants.

Thud, clank! Thud, clank, clank! The sound grew louder as they passed the larger adult elephants. Suddenly, Reba saw a baby elephant, hiding behind one of the giants, playing with a metal pedestal painted bright red. *Thud, clank!* Just like her little nephew would amuse himself by picking up a toy and dropping it to the floor, the baby elephant was scooping up the pedestal, lifting it in the air and dropping it to the earth. The animal kicked it with its feet, then twisted its trunk around the outside and flipped it over. *Thud, clank!* The metal toy bounced and rattled on the ground.

'*Ota* (that one),' said Ghosh, pointing at the baby elephant.

As they approached the elephant, it fanned out its broad flat ears and seemed to look at them mischievously.

'You'll take this one on your chest!' Ghosh said plainly.

Reba looked hard at the elephant, trying to get a sense for its personality. They would be partners in this after all. She was not so sure she trusted this little one. The elephant quickly stuck its trunk into a bucket of water, appearing to drink. Then it raised its trunk and sprayed water at the larger elephants. It seemed to be amusing itself to no end.

Its action could not help Reba wonder, *How can we trust this young animal to do what we want? What if it tries to scoop me up? Or kick me as if I am its feed bin.*

Suddenly the mahout appeared in front of them.

'How much does this one weigh?' Ghosh asked him.

'200 kilos.'

Reba looked at Ghosh, unsure if he thought this was very heavy or very light. But he gave a confident smile.

'It is basically the same weight as a motorcycle,' he reassured her.

She visibly relaxed. She had lifted a motorcycle dozens of times.

'The only difference is that the elephant will walk slowly. You will have to hold your breath and lift it for a little longer.'

The motorcycle comparison made it seem reasonable to Reba. But an elephant is a living being, totally in control of its own movements. Only the mahout has a close enough relationship with elephants to understand them.

A mahout usually worked with one elephant, or a very small group, developing a close bond.[160] He was in charge of cleaning, bathing and training the elephant for specific tasks. A mahout's day also consisted of treating the elephants for any illness, and feeding the elephants, sometimes making 'elephant sandwiches' of rice paddy, chickpea and molasses for treats. If the elephant was sold or gifted away, the mahout would be sold or gifted away along with the elephant. The mahout had to be present at any new situation, to read the reaction of the elephant and whether it vocalizes with any sign of aggression or is relaxed and curious. The mahout and the elephant have a deep relationship. They understand each other in any given situation.

Reba's heart rate was beating fast and her mind was becoming fuzzy. As her mind grew silent, she did not even feel the spray of water coming directly at her, straight from the elephant's trunk!

She was soaked but she felt nothing.

A small part of her recognized her Bishtuda's voice, yelling out in frustration. He too was now soaked with water. But to her, his voice was faint and mumbling, even as he stood by her side.

Slowly, the great experiment was conducted. The mahout brought the young elephant over to an open patch of ground. Reba spread out an old blanket they had brought with them so that she did not have to lay directly in the mud. Then she lay down on her back on the blanket. She could feel the wet

---

[160] Hannah S. Mumby, 'Mahout Perspectives on Asian Elephants and Their Living Conditions', 2019, https://www.ncbi.nlm.nih.gov/pmc/articles/PMC6912500/

and cool earth through the blanket underneath her. It smelled strongly of mud and animals. Ghosh laid a heavy wooden plank on her chest, far larger and heavier than the plank they used for the motorcycle stunt. This one needed to be wide enough to support the elephant. She was familiar with this feeling, the weight of the plank and the anticipation. She slowed down her breathing and waited for the big moment. She lay still. Calm.[161] Completely unperturbed.

It was difficult, perhaps impossible, to describe what went through her mind at this moment, when the massive creature stood on top of her. Her mind must have travelled to a different place—a place with no language, distant from her ordinary thinking mind.

While extreme situations cause some to howl in pain or scream at the top of their lungs, others simply cease to speak. They can no longer articulate what occurred. Much of what is beyond comprehension renders someone speechless.

While Reba lay under the plank in the mud, Ghosh and the mahout tried to convince the elephant to walk over her. The animal was not happy because the plank was unstable, and it was perfectly aware that it would be putting its weight *on top* of Reba. The elephant could sense danger in the act.

Finally, the elephant started to walk onto the wooden plank and over Reba's chest. Reba was familiar with this part of the stunt from her experience with motorcycles. It was actually easier in some ways than that stunt. The elephant approached much slower, so it was easier to know exactly when to inhale and hold her breath.

But Ghosh was right, it did last a lot longer.

---

[161] Rakshit, 'The Sport of Elephant Lifting', 253-264.

The motorcycle stunt was over in an instant. The elephant's weight pressed down on her for several seconds, maybe five or so. But when she was holding her breath in order to avoid being crushed and killed, a few seconds was a *very* long time.

That is when the world went silent. She left her body and mind as the pressure built on her slim body.

After the elephant had passed, Reba breathed, but the scent of the earth no longer registered.

The sound of the elephant's footsteps as it walked away were inaudible.

She slowly returned to her body and mind from far away. Ghosh came to her quickly, removing the plank from her chest and tossing it aside. He knelt by her head, grabbed her head with both hands and massaged it vigorously. He also shook her limbs. Then he picked up her hands and hoisted her up quickly and to her feet. She was standing, but had not yet fully returned to her body. She was not hearing the bustle around her, seeing clearly the ground in front, nor smelling the earth.

Until now she had often felt the rush of admiration from the crowds. She could sense their wonder as she balanced on one leg in her asanas. She was young, alert, daring and feeling it all. Where most would have frozen while standing in the spotlight, she took the adrenaline rush as a sign to step into the light and *perform*. She knew how fear felt like a big cloud of worry with stress as the side effect. She knew excitement came with opportunity. She could *feel*. That was, until what began as an ordinary day turned into the day far from ordinary. This was the day Reba's senses went dormant.

As Reba was standing again, Ghosh stared into her eyes with ferocity. He started quizzing her, 'How did you feel, Reba?'

As she returned into her body, his words came into focus. She scrunched her forehead as her eyes started shifting around again while her head pulsed. She mindlessly looked down and attempted to pull off some of the grass sticking to her skin, brushing away the chunks of mud.

Ghosh insisted, '*Kemon lagchilo, jokhon hatita chole gelo* (How did you feel when the elephant went over?)?'

Her eyes locked with Ghosh's.

'*Kichui bujhini* (I felt nothing at all),' she said.[162]

---

[162] Ibid.

14

The Show-stopper, the Guru And the Act

A Remarkable Feat of Strength, Beauty, Charisma And Skill

The news spread like wildfire. Circus companies from all over India were keen to know the young woman who could lift an elephant on her chest. Soon, Reba became the star attraction. Since the crowds were flocking to see her, many circus companies did not want to miss the opportunity to employ Reba as their star act.

One day, the impresario of the Great Bombay Circus came to Ghosh's college to hire her. He entered Byayamacharya Ghosh's office and took a seat.

'I've heard you have a woman student who can lift an elephant. A Miss Reba Rakshit?' he asked the Byayamacharya.

'Yes, I do.'

Ghosh had been expecting this interest. He was calm.

'I am in need of someone to perform this stunt in the Great Bombay Circus.'

Ghosh immediately declined his request and said, 'It is too risky to perform this stunt on a regular basis. Her delicate figure won't sustain such a thing.'

Ghosh was partially playing hardball, partially thinking out loud.

'Surely she can! She has already successfully completed the stunt!'

But Ghosh was firm.

'She is still a young girl, from a middle-class family and has not even completed her studies.'

The impresario reached across the shiny glass top of the big wooden desk, took Ghosh's hands in his own and pleaded, 'But it would be a huge loss if you refuse me. There is no other attraction in my circus this year. With no star performer, tickets will not sell. And the circus will fail!'

Ghosh was also a businessman himself. He was well aware of the difficulty of making ends meet as well as the thrill of success. This deal was a success for him just as much as for the circus.

'She will have to complete her studies first.'

'Of course …'

'She has just now taken her matriculate examinations and will take the BA once the results are released. You can include her stunt in your circus, but only when your company is touring Calcutta.'

The deal was sealed. Reba had a job with the Great Bombay Circus.[163] She was about to join the ranks of circus performers,

---

[163] Rakshit, 'The Sport of Elephant Lifting', 253-264.

characters who combined strength, beauty, charisma and a skill for performing impossible feats.

———•⚬⚬⚬•———

For nearly a century, the circus was one of the most popular enterprises in India with legendary performers that wowed audiences with their exceptional acts.[164] One great Indian strongman who combined feats of strength with yogic discipline was Kodi Ramamurthy Naidu, a performer from the turn of the twentieth century. He was known as the 'Indian Sandow', after the world famous German bodybuilder Eugen Sandow because of his strength and well-developed physique.[165] A large and powerful man, he was an accomplished wrestler and well recognized for his skill. He was also celibate, vegetarian and refrained from taking in any intoxicants, as physical and spiritual purity were important to many Indian physical culturists. Naidu performed incredible feats of strength like breaking a thick iron chain, lifting immense stones and, perhaps most incredible of all, supporting an elephant on his chest. He was also a yogi. He believed that his daily practice of pranayama and *dhyana* (meditation) was crucial to his success in the stunts.[166]

There was also the 'Indian Lady Sandow', Miss Tarabai.[167] Apart from being known for acrobatic skills and immense strength, she worked as an animal trainer. She owned the

---

[164] Anirban Ghosh, 'Who thought a sari-clad Bengali woman in slippers could terrify two man-eaters?' Scroll.in., 2017, https://scroll.in/magazine/822848/circus-women

[165] P.R. Nisha, *Jumbos and Jumping Devils: A Social History of Indian Circus* (New Delhi: Oxford University Press, 2020), 69.

[166] Ibid., 70.

[167] Ibid.

Tarabai Circus.[168] Thousands would flock to see her along with her troupe of fifty performers from both India and abroad. One article in the *Bombay Gazette* from 1917 proclaimed:

> Miss Tarabai's feats of strength are the most wonderful, startling and marvellous. Apart from its startling interest, the performance certainly has its educational value. All of her feats are extraordinarily unique—you must simply see them to admire them.[169]

Miss Tarabai was known to exercise every day, diligently choosing to use traditional Indian exercises like *dand, bethak* and *kasrath* selection.[170] Sandow's exercises, she believed, were good for shaping the physique but the Indian exercises were better overall. The usefulness of these exercises was not lost on many physical culturists. Wrestlers often incorporated them into their routines, building their upper body strength and coordination with the *dand*, a jack-knife push-up that is quite difficult for the arms and shoulders; developing their leg strength and flexibility with the *bethak*, a deep squatting motion that challenges balance and the strength of the knees and feet. And *kasrath*, a combined exercise of pull-ups and sit-ups was common in physical culture movements in the north, including Bengal.

In the generation prior to Reba, the circus arena was filled with talented Bengalis particularly Bhim Bhabani and Sushila Sundari both born in the late 1800s. The grandeur

---

[168] Ibid.
[169] Full Text of 'The Bombay Chronicle, 5 December 1917'. https://archive.org/stream/dli.granth.3821/3821_djvu.txt
[170] Nisha, *Jumbos and Jumping Devils*, p. 64.

of their stunts exceeded what might be expected from their short lives.

Bhim Bhabani was born Bhabendra Mohan Saha ten years before the turn of the twentieth century.[171] He was a *pehlwan*, a wrestler. The practice gave him immense strength. He started his training under Khudiram Babu, founder of the Simla Byayam Samity.[172] Then his large frame became increasingly filled out with thick muscles under the tutelage of well-respected Khetu Guha.[173] Many young wrestlers travelled from outside Calcutta to train at his akhara under his guidance. For example, Gobor Guha, who trained a young Swami Vivekananda, also frequented his akhara.[174] Bhim Bhabani then continued with the Indian bodybuilder 'Professor Rammurty' who started an Indian circus company.

Bhim Bhabani travelled the subcontinent performing remarkable feats of strength. He could stop an automobile on its tracks, support a massive stone weighing many thousand pounds on his chest and move a huge barrel with a dozen people sitting on top by clenching it with his teeth.[175] Or so the legend goes. His immensely popular shows drew large adoring crowds.[176] But most importantly, he was the first Bengali to support the weight of an elephant on his chest. But then, at the young age of thirty-two, just when his remarkable strength

---

[171] Abhijit Gupta, 'Man Who Lifted Elephants', Telegraph India Online, 2010, https://www.telegraphindia.com/west-bengal/man-who-lifted-elephants/cid/1272354

[172] Raha et al., *Mapping the Path to Maturity: A Connected History of Bengal and the North-East* (London: Routledge, 2017).

[173] Gupta, 'Man Who Lifted Elephants'.

[174] Mapping the Path to Maturity.

[175] Gupta, 'Man Who Lifted Elephants'.

[176] *Byayam Charcha*. National Library. Kolkata.

was at its peak, Bhim Bhabani passed away. Undoubtedly, his extraordinary physical feats took a severe toll on his body.

Sushila Sundari, 'Beautiful Sushila', was a contemporary of Bhim Bhabani. She was born in 1879 in Rambagan, Calcutta. She was the first Indian woman to perform in a circus, where she famously worked with Royal Bengal tigers. *The Englishman* newspaper commented on her powerful demeanour:

> What impresses the observer most are the performances of Miss Sushila and the two Royal Bengal tigers. Hindu women are notoriously most timid but in the person of Sushila, there is one who with the utmost fearlessness, enters the den of the two apparently savage beasts without either whip or any other defensive appliance.[177]

Besides her acts with the tigers, Sushila was known for her equestrian skills. She could not only effortlessly ride bareback, but also sometimes backwards at high speeds. However, she too lived a short life, passing away just two years after Bhim Bhabani, in 1924. Her acts were impressive and admired by crowds, but she struggled to gain acceptance as a woman in the male-dominated performance ring. She grieved about this until her dying day.[178]

Sushila Sundari was trained for the circus by the legendary ringmaster Priyanath Bose, Bengal's first proprietor of the

---

[177] Aastha Gandhi, 'From Postcolonial to Neoliberal' Performance Matters, 2018, https://performancematters-thejournal.com/index.php/pm/article/view/140

[178] 'About the frontpiece', *Byayam Charcha*. National Library. Kolkata.

circus.[179] He founded the Great Bengal Circus in 1877, impressed by the international circuses that had been visiting India. England's Wilson's Great World Circus and Chiarini's Italian Circus would come to town, covering the parade grounds with tents and excitement.[180] Bose noticed that while the acrobatics, strength stunts and magic tricks were impressive, the circuses were missing animal performances.[181] Over time, Bose worked animal acts into his circus. He toured all over the Indian subcontinent, giving outstanding performance in every state. The Maharaja of Rewa gifted Priyanath Bose two Royal Bengal tigers, named Lakshmi and Narayan, for the Great Bengal Circus.[182]

For performers, the circus was about survival in more ways than one since many of their acts were difficult and even dangerous. After all, a stunt with no risk of injury was unremarkable and unexciting. So they were constantly navigating their need to make a living, which they did by performing remarkable feats, with the inherent risks to their health and life.

As the circus increased in popularity, there was not much escape from it. Several different companies travelled from town to town to put on shows, and with this came an excitement about continuously pushing the barriers of what the human body could do. How stunning, shocking, jaw-dropping and dazzling could the performances be? Sometimes it was about nationalism and a sense of pride. Could the sense of strength

---

[179] Ghosh, 'Who thought a sari-clad Bengali woman in slippers could terrify two man-eaters?'
[180] *Byayam Charcha*. National Library. Kolkata.
[181] 'Circus in Bengal', *Byayam Charcha*. National Library. Kolkata.
[182] *Byayam Charcha*. National Library. Kolkata.

required in the strongman feats, and the power and exertion in the wrestling acts display a sense of national fitness, of Indian physical prowess?

Circuses toured around Bengal, going from the rural areas to the cities and back. The circus was a source of dignity for those who watched. The spectators were extremely proud to see the strength and stamina of the Bengalis.[183] Even Swami Vivekananda raved about the importance of the circus, claiming that it was not just a source of entertainment, but also a source of pride—a way to promote skill in physical culture. Locals embraced the spectacle starting from when the first show was staged in Bengal—at the Maidan in 1899. The circuses of the era had many wealthy and royal patrons.[184]

The circus also had a political role to play. Like the samitis, they were gathering places for social action, for example, proceeds were collected for donation to local famine relief and charity. The fact that the circus attracted political figures helped establish and promote it as a place for the young to be inspired to take up physical culture. If the youth developed their skill, strength and physique, they had the power to influence society.

The phenomenon of the circus arrived in the subcontinent at a time of many other shake-ups. Just like yoga and modernity, physical culture and entertainment were shifting and gaining a new meaning. There were many circus companies popping up around the turn of the twentieth century and in the decades that followed. The Jumbo Circus, International Circus,

---

[183] Amitava Chatterjee, 'Exhibiting Masculine Identity through Circus in Colonial Bengal', *Studies in People's History* 2, issue 2 (2015). https://journals.sagepub.com/doi/full/10.1177/2348448915600943
[184] Ibid.

Gemini Circus, Great Bombay Circus and others hung their banners on tents all across India.

The tents pitched in the wide open green space of the Maidan in the centre of Calcutta gave a temporary home to circus companies from far and near. When the Great Bombay Circus first performed in Calcutta in 1901 to enthusiastic crowds, *The Bengalee* declared: 'The gymnastics and acrobatic feats of the troupe were excellent and worth revisiting'.[185]

Reba's first professional performance under her contract came when The Great Bombay Circus returned to Calcutta. The company promoted the performance from Maniktala in the north to Alipore in the south. Posters were hung all around the city so as to make them impossible to miss; cycle vans made their way north and south, east towards Salt Lake and west across the river to Howrah with news of the event blasting from their megaphones; handbills were distributed in railway stations and newspapers ran ads as follows:

Great Bombay Circus
A busy week! Every day at 3 o' clock and 6 o'clock.

Impressive sights! The word is out in high praise of the performance.[186]

---

[185] Ibid.
[186] *Jugantar*, Vol.18, Issue 94 (22 December 1954), British Library, EAP262/1/2/18/353, https://eap.bl.uk/archive-file/EAP262-1-2-18-353

Promotion by word of mouth reached far and wide, so much so that the circus tent was packed almost daily. The stage was set especially for Reba's elephant stunt. To accommodate such a large animal was no small feat. The elephant needed a place backstage to wait before its entrance, the door into the tent and onstage needed to be large enough to accommodate the tall animal, and the ring had to be large and with even footing.

Backstage, Reba readied herself. As she listened to the humming of the massive crowd and the happy melody of the band, she felt her nerves prickle through her. The cool December air from outside began to warm with the presence of the gathering. The lion was roaming around. The tiger too. The trapeze performers were stretching their bodies in order to warm up. The other performers were dressing in the corners, putting on their costumes and make-up in front of small portable mirrors, and making themselves ready for the stage.

A huge selling point for the public was the chance to see the wild, powerful, stunning animals up close. After Independence, the elephant was a draw since it was a part of India's post-colonial national identity. Prime Minister Jawaharlal Nehru, perhaps in an effort to secure diplomatic relations, gifted elephants to zoos around the world.[187]

The circus companies owned their own animals, which complicated the dynamics with hired circus performers like Reba. Since each company had its own elephant, the behaviour and temperament of each was different.[188] So often Reba did

---

[187] Nikhil Menon, 'India's History of Elephant Diplomacy', *The Caravan*, 2019, https://caravanmagazine.in/lede/india-history-elephant-diplomacy
[188] 'Wild Personalities: Elephant Edition', Smithsonian's National Zoo and Conservation Biology Institute, 2018, https://nationalzoo.

not know what to expect because some elephants were bold, others shy; some were quite laid-back, others very curious or even short-tempered. Hence, each time Reba performed the act with an elephant, her life was on the line.

In a concealed corner, Reba undraped her saree and pulled on her costume. She stepped into her leotard one foot at a time, being careful it did not drag in the dirt. She tugged gently at the shiny fabric, slipping it up her body. She pulled it up past her long legs until it held her torso tightly. She liked the golden sheen of the leotard and the way the thin straps rested on her shoulders. She was going shopping in New Market more frequently now to order new costumes. Kalam was her preferred tailor. It was worth her time and effort to weave through the crowded lanes of New Market to place orders for new dresses and costumes for her performances. Every part of show business had to be looked into and perfected. As she was beginning to perform more and more, she needed many options to pick from and Kalam never disappointed.

Once she was dressed, she braided and pinned her hair so it framed her face. She made sure everything was in place—costume, hair, make-up.

The small leotard hugged her torso but left her arms and legs completely exposed. It usually shocked the crowd to see a young Bengali woman dressed as she was! But she was a performer on the stage and this was the realm of magic and flare, not a time for societal norms or modesty. Still, she felt self-conscious about her costume. She was a daughter of the soil, prone to the same cultural demands as her sister, mother

---

si.edu/conservation-ecology-center/news/wild-personalities-elephant-edition and friends. Then again, the crowds of people had paid to watch *her*. In some ways she felt powerful, as if she was in charge. She was the object of the audience's praise. But in other ways she felt powerless, like a disposable object of their entertainment; something they could feast their eyes on; something that made them gasp with anticipation, shock and excitement; something that gave them a story to tell in their own social circles.

From backstage, Reba could hear that the show was beginning. The band began playing the overture, energetic and rhythmic music that marked the start, grabbing people's attention, encouraging them to take their seats and quiet down. One by one the actors took the stage—acrobats, trapeze artists, tiger. Then came an intermission and finally, the performances of the second act.

As the show neared its climax, it was Reba's turn. She confidently pushed through the curtain at the back onto the stage and walked to the centre. The spectators felt a mix of emotions—excitement because this was the act they were waiting for; surprise at how young and beautiful Reba was; shock at her small and revealing costume; and exhilaration that this woman would place her body underneath the weight of an elephant.

With her hands at her chest in namaskar, she bowed her head to the audience.

As soon as she lifted her head, the crowd's cheers turned into gasps and disbelief as the elephant entered the ring.

It began to circle around the centre of the platform. The graceful move of the majestic and massive creature was impressive. Its thick and tall legs carried its enormous body; its soft feet spread with each step; its large ears flapped and rolled in the air as it paced.

The music picked up its energy, exciting everyone in the tent.

Sitting in the audience was the Speaker of the West Bengal Legislative Assembly, Shaila Mukherjee, who had come to watch the circus on that its first performance. As Reba began to lie down in the centre of the stage, Mukherjee approached Ghosh frantically with a worried look on his face.[189] Ghosh was standing attentively at the side of the ring and watching Reba prepare herself for the act. He heard Mukherjee behind him say, 'Don't do this event! Let this poor girl go home!'

In the ring, Reba was stiffening her body in preparation. The stagehands brought out the heavy wooden plank and carefully placed it on her chest. The elephant's pace was quickening, around and around the ring, always moving. Soon the mahout would make a change in direction, guiding the big animal towards the centre and up and over Reba's chest. Ghosh kept turning his head to look over his shoulder, pulled between the anxious demands of Shaila Babu and Reba. He could not afford to miss his cue, the most vital moment of the act.

The moment was close.

Reba took a deep, full breath.

The elephant and mahout paced around and around.

Then she emptied her breath halfway. Just as she did, Ghosh signalled to the mahout. In a flash, the elephant changed course from circling around the outside to cut across the centre of the ring.

Reba held her breath half in, half out. Her body was solid.

The elephant lifted its right, front leg up and onto the wood. She felt the pillows between the plank and her body flatten completely.

---

[189] Rakshit, 'The Sport of Elephant Lifting', 253–264.

At that point, Ghosh's attention was interrupted again. Mukherjee pleaded in his ear, 'Take the elephant down! Take the elephant down! Take the elephant down!'

But the act was already underway.

Reba was suspended in time by the stillness of her breath, hovering in between success and failure. In her case, in between life and death.

The audience also held its breath, becoming completely silent in the suspense. All eyes were fully stuck on the elephant and Reba, mouths open wide in awe. Collectively, the onlookers leaned in to watch each moment unfold. It was both fast—it took just a few moments for the elephant to make its way across Reba's chest—and slow. The atmosphere was pregnant with disbelief, fear and anxiety.

Once the elephant had gone over, step by step, and down the wooden plank, Reba felt the pressure on her body ease and her breath return. Her muscles relaxed slightly, but stayed firm until the wooden plank was lifted off her. Once the plank and pillows were removed, Reba was pulled to her feet.

She was in a trance-like state—still suspended in time, hazy.

The immense pressure of the act, physical and mental, pushed her mind and body into a different realm. She turned to the audience.

She bowed in namaskar, this time as though hypnotized.

With her body taking over, she exited one foot in front of the other with Ghosh by her side.

The crowd erupted in the sounds of relief, shock, joy and admiration. The cheers echoed behind her as she disappeared from the stage.

Whether it was the Speaker of the assembly or members of her family, someone always voiced their fear and horror at the danger of what Reba was doing. However, what they were unaware of is that Reba was a strong, young woman. And she was a star whose popularity increased one show after another; one act at a time. Once the word started travelling about her act, there was no stopping it. The circus ring was built for a star like Reba. So the show continued every day, twice a day, three times on the weekends. Reba performed with her guru by her side and the elephant on her chest.

15

The Show Never Stops ...

The Day It Almost Did

The Great Bombay Circus stayed on in Calcutta for two months over the winter. Although Ghosh directed the performances, it was Reba who was in the contract with the circus. Her act was in such demand that she soon had positions with other eminent circuses like Kamala, Oriental, Gemini and International.

The money started to add up. A hundred and twenty-five rupees for weekday shows and 200 rupees for the weekend shows. For a young woman in a young India, both the pay and prestige were considerable. Because the circus was in Calcutta, there was no travel, food or lodging expenses.

The shows were packed with eager audiences. Aggressive marketing and publicity by word of mouth made it a grand success. Soon esteemed figures started to take note as well. It had the likes of King Mahendra Bir Bikram Shah Dev of Nepal attend Reba's performance.

Ghosh received letters of admiration for the work he was doing in perfecting such talent. Governor of West Bengal Kailash Nath Katju praised the performances of several of Ghosh's students, writing, 'I have had the pleasure of seeing the demonstrations of their skill and physical fitness.'[190] He was particularly impressed with the tumbling and horizontal bar display of all-India gymnastics champion Dulal Kanji.

But he went on, 'I have also seen with admiration the skill displayed by Kumari Labanya Palit and Kumari Reba Rakshit, Sri Gouri Shanker Mukherjee and Sri Bishnu Charan Ghosh in Sharp Shooting Exercises … Sri Bishnu Charan Ghosh deserves encouragement and congratulations for the work he is doing in promoting the cause of physical fitness among the youth of Bengal.'

After performing with the Kamala Circus on a particularly grand evening in Cooch Behar, Reba performed privately for its royal family headed by Maharaja Kumar Jagaddipendra Narayan brother of Rajmata Gayatri Devi. The Cooch Behar royal family were great admirers of Reba.

In the winter of 1957, when the circus was back in Calcutta, Jyotsna and Swapan came to see her perform. Swapan was excited to see the animals more than anything else, and he was happy that he would see his mashi and an elephant in the same act.

As evening came, crowds filled the huge striped tent. Small barefoot children pressed their eyes to any hole or tear in the tent, hoping to get a glimpse of a mighty tiger or flipping trapeze artist.

---

[190] Letter courtesy of Romit Banerjee from his private collection.

Poking her head out from behind the curtain, Reba scanned the audience, looking into the sea of people for her family. This was a special night. They were here, ready to bear witness to her impossible feat. She saw them, right there in the front row. Her Bishtuda had found a spot for them close to the ring. Jyotsna was looking right at her. As their eyes locked together, it was clear—this was not yet a time to celebrate her success. First she had to *survive* her act. This finale act was the very reality Reba carried on her back. The weight of it hung on her shoulders day in and day out. Tonight, just like other important nights, adrenaline coursed through her veins, as she felt the pressure to succeed.

Then the act was introduced.

As Reba looked from behind the curtain, she shifted her eyes from Jyotsna's down to little Swapan's. He was grinning with joy, seeing his mashi under the big top. However, Swapan's grin immediately transformed into a look of terror as he stared wide-eyed at the elephant entering from the opposite side of the stage. It was larger than he could have ever imagined. Little Swapan tugged at his mother's arm, jumping a few times into the air with enthusiasm.

'*Dakho*, Ma! *Dakho* (look)!' But his mother's eyes did not move towards the elephant. Instead they stayed on Reba and her slender frame, still partially hidden backstage. *This was a bad idea*, she thought. *Coming here, watching this.* Jyotsna turned to look behind her, scanning the crowd and the tent, trying to find a way out.

The excitement dropped and settled into a pit in her stomach.

Her heart was beating punches against her chest, heat was building on her skin.

Finally, panic set in. But it was no use looking for a way out. There was a huge crowd behind her. The tent was packed tightly. They simply could not escape. There was nothing to do but wait. They would have to watch the stunt. But she had come to see her sister triumph, not perish! Desperately, she grabbed Swapan's hand, chanting help from God.

'*Thakur, Thakur ...*'

They watched with dread as the stunt was introduced. In the centre of the ring was a heavy plank of wood, resting over a pivot point creating a see-saw. Before the actual stunt was performed, odd objects supported the wooden plank. Old petroleum cans were piled underneath as the pivot for the see-saw. But once the stunt began, *Reba's body* would take their place.

The mahout began to circle the elephant in tight loops around the ring. Around they went; he instructed the animal to walk '*amar kachhe* (close to me)'. Then, he guided the giant creature into the centre, towards the see-saw. But each time the elephant approached the plank of wood, it stepped sideways to avoid the unsteady wooden see-saw. The mahout needed to get the elephant comfortable with moving from stable to shifting ground.

The elephant had to keep moving. It had to know that it could not pause. If it got in the habit of stopping and standing still during the stunt—once its weight was on Reba—her life would be over. It was as simple as that.

The mahout continued. After a few more circles, he again led the elephant to the centre. This time, the elephant took a step onto the plank of wood. From backstage, Reba could see the inquisitive way the elephant approached it. It was calm, playful, yet unsure.

Finally, the elephant made its way across the plank of wood.

Thik achhe, Reba thought. *Keep moving.*

But just as the thought popped into her mind, a crushing sound pierced the air. The weight of the elephant had flattened all of the steel cans that were lying underneath the wooden plank. Those were the cans that were a stand in for *her*.

This is all part of the act, Reba reminded herself. *It's all for show.*

As the elephant stepped off of the wood and resumed circling the outside of the ring, the assistants raced towards the centre to set up the real act.

Reba watched this unfold. As her time approached, her adrenaline lost its edge. The calmness of her mind overpowered the anxious anticipation. Her trained sense of one-pointed concentration (ekagrata) and control of her nervous system kicked in. As she focused her mind on what was to come, her senses quieted. Her gaze became sharp, laser-focused.

Then came the numbness.

'Reba!' Ghosh called out. 'It's time! *Cholo* (let's go)!'

'Here I am, ready.'

She was already making her entrance.

'Now stay calm, it's just as we've practised.'

'*Haa, haa. Ami jani.*'

She called out in response but the noise of the crowd drowned her voice. 'It's just as we've practised.'

Reba pushed through the curtain and began to walk towards the centre of the ring. She stopped in the middle, put her hands together and bowed to the audience. Then she gave a huge smile to project confidence!

Slowly the look on little Swapan's face began to change. A look of awe changed to confusion, then to fear. The calculations in little Swapan's mind were simply not adding up.

Mashi = *choto* (small).

Hati (elephant) = *boro* (big*)*.

Aunty is so small and the elephant is so big! Surely, she will be crushed under its weight. Jyotsna and Swapan stood in the audience, their eyes glued on the action in the ring.

In the ring, Reba knelt down. She pressed her forehead into the earth and rested her palms there. Thakur, thakur, she repeated, turning herself over to God, just as she always did. *Don't let this go wrong tonight, just not in front of my family.* She sensed Ghosh shift his weight, eager for her to stand up and get into place. She felt all eyes resting on her back.

With that, she stood tall.

The elephant was still circling, its footsteps and her heart were beating in the same stride. In the middle of the ring were two mattresses. She sat down on them and stretched out her legs. She lay back, her head resting on a pillow. Ghosh picked up another pillow and handed it to the stagehand. Ghosh and the stagehand, each with a pillow in hand, went to either side of Reba and carefully pressed the pillows next to her abdomen. One more was placed underneath her legs.

Ghosh gestured to the men carrying the large wooden plank. It weighed 370 kilos.[191] He motioned for them to lay it on top of her. They moved in an awkward sideways walk. It took six of them just to carry it. The pillows were placed just right. If all went well, the plank would teeter-totter just so, rolling over Reba with each step the elephant took. To be sure the placement was correct—taking care here was a matter of life or death—the stagehand climbed on the plank, legs wide. He shifted right and left, the plank rolling over Reba's chest in a semicircular motion.

---

[191] 'Elephant Girl', *The Times of India* (15 April 2001), B7.

The pace of the elephant had slowed slightly now as it rounded the turn, beginning to face Reba and the ramp it would walk across. Ghosh knelt low, hovering over Reba, confident in both his training and her preparation.

Swapan grabbed his mother's hand and squeezed it harder and harder with each step the elephant took—his little fingers digging into Jyotsna's hand. Just as the elephant placed one foot on the wood, Swapan pressed his eyes shut. He could not bear to watch. Even with a front row seat, he would not see the first moments of the stunt. Despite Ghosh's efforts to get him the best view in the house, he could only bear to watch.

Swapan heard the mummers in the crowd fade to a hush.

Then silence.

Then the creaking of wood underneath the weight of the elephant as it placed a foot on the wooden plank. A quarter of the elephant's weight now rested on Reba's chest.

This time the silence was broken by the mahout, urging the elephant, 'Come on, girl, come on!'

Moments felt like a lifetime as the elephant got all four feet on the plank and it slowly became level, parallel to the ground, resting on Reba's chest.

The entire weight of the elephant now rested on her.

The mahout held a hook in his hand and prodded the elephant to continue. If the elephant stalled now, Reba's life would be over. She would be crushed just like the cans were a minute earlier. *One second could be the difference between life and death.*

Reba's mind went blank. She lost all perception of what was going on, her senses completely numb.

The elephant took just two more steps as a second stagehand ran to the back end of the wooden plank. He grabbed it by the edge and lifted it up in the air, coaxing the elephant down the ramp and relieving some of the weight from Reba. Ghosh stood still, waiting for his part—*the revival.*

Just as soon as the elephant had walked off, the stagehands rushed towards Reba. Quickly, they lifted the plank off her. One took her left leg, another her right. Ghosh bent down, taking her cheeks in his hands. All three of them jiggled, patted and shook Reba, willing her body to circulate its blood once again.

She was silent, she was still.

Despite their revival efforts, she stayed lying on her back, without any movement at all. The crowd did not know whether to cheer or pray.

By that time, little Swapan had opened his eyes. He saw the crowd around Reba and knew the stunt was over. But what he could not see was the signs of life in his mashi. Still squeezing his mother's hand, he looked up, 'Ma! Is mashi okay?'

Jyotsna stood in shock and disbelief. If Reba was okay, it was an act of magic. Pure magic that transcended all laws of the physical world. *And if Reba wasn't okay…*

Jyotsna and Swapan stood among the thousands looking on waiting to find out what fate lay ahead. The stagehands continued trying to revive Reba. The crowd waited in breathless anticipation to see if she had survived. Every time, Reba too waited to see if she had survived.

Although she was Reba the *lucky one*, at any moment her luck could run out.

But not tonight.

The stunt was a success.

Reba was pulled to her feet. As she stood and bowed with her hands at her chest, Jyotsna and Swapan cheered along with the rest, their awe and excitement mixed with a feeling of relief. They had thought it would be pure entertainment to see their own family member cheat death, but it was not the same as watching a stranger, who could appear somehow less human and more otherwordly. Watching her popularity grow was exciting, but witnessing the constant threat to her life was unsettling. And the worst was yet to come.

16

Fighting Hate, Malice And Violence with Aplomb

The Pride of Bengal under Threat

Not everyone was happy with Reba's growing fame. Rumours started to circulate about her; there were vague suggestions of impropriety, bad behaviour and even questions of identity. Nobody could identify the source of the gossip, but the chatter was everywhere. Some people were disturbed by Reba's small revealing costume that left most of her body on display. She had beauty and elegance and also strength. Some thought she was not a woman and that her physical strength was against the natural laws of femininity. Although people paid to see her beauty, strength and courage night after night, her act challenged what was culturally acceptable. Standing with so many eyes falling upon her, with her bare legs and shiny fabric tightly hugging her curves was too much for some.

Some would say, '*Eta apasanskriti* (it is culture)!'

Reba was a woman who was not only unmarried, but also living independently and earning her own living. Since she was not caring for a home like a traditional Bengali wife, some would strongly object to such a lifestyle, '*Eta toh mene newa jaay na* (this is not acceptable)!'

Some were also envious of her success, which was understandable, as she was earning a good living and her fame grew by the day. So, Reba was a natural target of a lot of criticism.

Although many women were performing in the circus and in films and theatre by the 1950s, her choices rattled a lot of people. Reba was not in films at this point and sometimes envied the protection that the big screen offered to the actresses. They did not have to perform their feats live in front of people. She was not Fearless Nadia in *Hunterwali*, who had the protection of the screen to ease the audience's reactions to her fearless stunts and displays of strength. Reba was a *bhodro barir meye*, a typical Bengali middle-class woman, and exuding such confidence, charisma and sensuality in such a public space (and in person no less!) went against the grain.

Ghosh was always by her side too. He trained her and oversaw her performances. He trained many others, of course, but Reba was becoming one of his big stars and required a lot of his attention which did not go down well with many of his students.

The type of relationship Ghosh and Reba had was becoming more and more common as the twentieth century crept on. Girls and young women were becoming singers, dancers, actors and performers, and they usually had a strong male figure who trained, managed and oversaw every aspect of their lives. The growing film industry in Bombay was importing talent from various cities—Calcutta being one of them. Calcutta became a centre for young girls who were being groomed for performing careers. Although Reba was becoming a star, she was promoted as just an average young Bengali woman because the circus promoters thought this made her more appealing. Yet, she was *not* just an average Bengali woman. She was performing feats many would not even dream of! This constant friction between the image of ordinary accessibility and an extraordinary performer of unimaginable power grabbed the public's attention, and sometimes unsettled them.

Furthermore, Reba was guarded and inaccessible as Ghosh was always by her side. She could not be reached easily, despite being so visible to the public.

The Maidan was again bustling with big bursts of energy. The circus run was in full swing. Nestled in between ads for popular films like *20,000 Leagues under the Sea* and *Mahanisha*, the Great Bombay Circus advertised Reba as their most impressive act:

Great Bombay Circus
Saturday, Sunday: 3, 5 and 9 p.m.
The pride of Bengal Kumari Reba Rakshit lifting an elephant on her chest!
Fierce lions and tigers playing and roaming freely throughout the open premise
And also many new sports, comedy, exercises
Howrah Maidan[192]

---

[192] *Jugantar*, Vol.19, Issue 75 (3 December 1955), British Library, EAP262/1/2/19/335, https://eap.bl.uk/archive-file/EAP262-1-2-19-335.

By now, Reba was comfortable in the routine of the day. She arrived at the circus grounds with Ghosh and went directly to her changing area to prepare. She changed out of her saree and slipped off her canvas shoes, putting on her leotard. Sometimes, before the performances began, she would take promotional photographs for the circus, a newspaper or magazine story. She might wear her costume or even one of the new small swimsuits that were split into two pieces. Although these types of outfits were becoming more common in films, they were quite rare in real life. Just a few years before when Nalini Jaywant wore a swimsuit in the movie *Sangram*, it caused quite a stir. It was this type of suit that Reba's costumes emulated—thin straps and a V-neck cut across her chest.

Revealing costumes were common for both male and female performers. The entertainers often had beautiful, well-developed bodies and displaying these added to their attractiveness. Even Ghosh, at his school, sometimes dressed his students in skimpy garments to show off their toned muscular bodies. Two decades prior, he had photographed young Buddha Bose in a tiny costume, covering only what was absolutely essential. Bose performed asanas for the camera, and these nearly naked pictures were published beyond Indian shores. In a costume like that, each muscle was clearly on display to the audience. Sometimes these short pants were in leopard print as a mark of showmanship. Hence, it was not unusual for Reba to don a revealing costume for performances.

Once Reba was dressed and it was her time to perform, everything moved on cue. The music kicked in playing popular film songs which made the audience clap and sing along, Ghosh walked out in his freshly crisped suit and shiny shoes, and together they prepared for the act.

Each stunt had to be set up in a perfect series of events. The ground had to be flat. Any unevenness would make the pressure on Reba's body uneven. This could be deadly once the elephant's weight was on her. Then a mattress had to be laid flat. This provided just a hint of cushion which absorbed and distributed the weight of Reba's body evenly. If she were to lay on the solid ground, Reba would be flattened instead of the mattress. Then, on top of the mattress lay Reba. On top of Reba, more pillows to absorb and evenly spread the weight of the wooden plank.

But that day something did not feel right.

She was used to having nothing below her but the padding of the mattress, with the firm ground below that. This time there was a strange, unfamiliar pressure in her back. A pebble perhaps? Or was it one rock? Several? Uneven ground?

She calmed herself. *No, it's nothing. The ground has been inspected. We have done this a hundred times.*

The next set of stagehands entered, carrying the heavy wooden plank. Reba could tell they were approaching because the crowd's intensity picked up. It took two men to carry it, one on each side. The weight of the wood was substantial, around 40 kilograms. It had to be heavy and solid enough to support the elephant. If the foot of the elephant was placed on anything thin, it would crack like kindling in an instant. Carefully they bent over and, under Ghosh's guidance, placed the wooden plank on top of Reba, covering her chest and most of her legs. Her head stuck out so that the audience could see her the whole time. It was like a see-saw with Reba at the centre. The weight of the plank alone was enough to cause an untrained person to panic. The cheers and excitement grew as the stunt got closer.

The strange pressure on Reba's back was more obvious now that the weight of the plank was on top of her.

Something isn't right.

Instead of an evenly dispersed push of her body into the mattress below, there were several points where she could feel resistance pressing up against her back.

Her mind started racing. Her heartbeat quickened in her chest. She shifted her body slightly this way and that, trying to relieve the pressure or get a better sense of what was there.

But she could not relieve it. There was definitely an unexpected object underneath her.

The act was underway and something was *wrong*.

She was sure of it now.

How would she get her Bishtuda's attention? Her arms were pinned down by the weight of the plank, and she was entirely immobile for the duration of the stunt. While he kept a keen eye on the act, everything *looked* correct from the outside. It was only that it *felt* wrong to her.

Reba tried to call out.

It was difficult to take a deep breath because the wooden plank was pressing down on her. She yelled, but it was only a half-yell. The sound was swallowed up by the noise and energy in the tent.

She heard the elephant pacing around and knew she had a matter of seconds before it would step onto the plank. If the 2,000 kilos of the fully grown elephant pressed her into the earth with this strange pressure in her back, she could easily be seriously injured or killed.

She had to focus and she had to do it quickly.

'Wait! Something is wrong!' she yelled. But her voice was nothing against the roaring of the crowd and the piping music.

'Stop, stop! Stop!'

But no one heard her.

The crowd was getting louder and louder as the elephant circled. They knew the stunt was close. They started clapping together in rhythm, drowning out every other sound in the tent.

It was then that Ghosh inspected everything for the final time. He noticed Reba's chin was slightly turned to the side.

That's not right, he thought.

Her neck had to remain perfectly straight so that the pressure never went sideways.

He looked closer and saw her mouth moving.

She was trying to say something. She looked afraid, not her usual calm focus.

'Wait! Stop!' she cried out again. This time Ghosh saw her mouth move even though he could not hear her. He hurried towards her, quickly moving from the edge of the ring to the centre. He knelt down by her head.

'Reba, what is it?'

'Stop, stop,' was all she could manage as she lay trapped under the pillows and wooden plank.

By now Ghosh knew of Reba's unwavering determination and courage. This was a necessary trait of anyone he agreed to train. She had performed this stunt hundreds of times. She would not stop unless something was actually wrong. Ghosh quickly snapped into action without a moment's hesitation. He immediately motioned to the stagehands to remove the plank, lifting it off of her body. In a moment, the pillows were picked up and removed.

Ghosh grabbed Reba's sweaty hands and pulled her to her feet.

We must always be performing, Reba thought. *The audience cannot know that something has gone wrong.*

She instantly turned to the audience, raised both of her arms and waved happily, a huge smile on her face. And then she abruptly turned and exited the ring, leaving the crowd baffled.

The elephant which was circling the ring was escorted out.

The Master of Ceremonies, without dropping a beat, improvised an explanation to the crowd about the dangers and difficulties of the show.

Ghosh exited the ring with a slower, confident pace. He did not want it to appear to the crowd like Reba was a coward, or they were not going to complete the performance.

Once he was backstage, Ghosh approached Reba, who was visibly shaken and was pacing in a small circle, with a terror-stricken face.

'Reba, *ki holo* (what happened)?'

'Something was wrong. I know it. I could feel it.'

Although her heart was still racing, she felt a lot calmer now that she was out of the situation.

'Nonsense!'

Ghosh had overseen the whole thing. Nothing was out of the ordinary. Nothing was wrong.

'Just check! It was uneven, there was some type of pressure. Perhaps a rock or something we missed …'

Her voice trailed off, uncertain about what it could be.

Ghosh turned and walked back into the ring. By now the audience was starting to filter out in frustration, after a very anticlimactic finish to the night. Reba's stunt was the last one; there was nothing else to show. While the Master of Ceremonies had tried to fill time to reduce any disappointment, it became clear the show was over. No elephant stunt would take place.

Ghosh walked to the centre where the mattress was still resting on the ground. Around the edges of the ring, stagehands were beginning to clean up in preparation for the next day's performance. Reba tentatively entered behind him, not sure if she should walk all the way to the centre. She was still haunted by what she had felt, deeply embarrassed that she had let the audience down and aware of the spectators filtering out. Some were turning back to see what was happening, unsure whether they should leave or not.

Ghosh circled the mattress. *It looks absolutely fine,* he thought. *What is wrong? This is the same set-up that is always used.*

He picked up a corner of the mattress and looked underneath it.

The ground was smooth and even.

Just to be sure he motioned to the stagehands to pick up the other corners and move the mattress off to the side so that they could inspect the ground more closely. He bent down, putting his face close to the earth, scanning the area. There was not a pebble to be found. Nothing was there that could have disrupted the act. They picked up the mattress once again and moved it back to the centre.

Then he saw it.

What on earth …?

On the mattress, there was a small section of stitching that appeared different from the rest. Around the edge, the thick thread that bound the top to the side was worn evenly, except for one section that looked like the stitching was newer, the thread cleaner. The edges of the fabric were frayed and pulled.

It looked as though the fabric had been cut and resewn.

Ghosh's eyes widened in shock and anger. Suddenly, he yelled in full voice, 'Cut it! Cut it! Open this up! Give me a knife!'

A stagehand pulled a small knife out of his pocket and handed it to Ghosh who ripped open the newly placed threads. He grabbed the two ends of fabric and pulled them apart strongly, ripping the mattress open.

Reba walked closer, still unsure of whether or not she wanted to look. Then she heard audible gasps from the stagehands looking on. Ghosh was now completely shocked by what lay in front of him.

Nestled within the padding of the cushion, was a circular knife.

Ghosh stared at it in utter horror and surprise. Slowly he stood up, keeping his eyes fixed on the metallic sheen of the knife. His chin tucked into his chest, eyes gazing down, he stood perfectly still. The world stopped around him.

Reba, still standing back, realized something had happened. What was causing this reaction in her Bishtuda? She had to know.

Slowly she walked towards the centre of the ring, leaned around Ghosh and looked. When she saw the shiny blade of the knife, her heart stopped. She did not make a sound, but heard a thundering boom in her head.

It was then that they both realized the extent of the situation. Had the act continued, the weight of the elephant would have pressed Reba's body down onto the knife. It would have pushed all the way into her, stabbing her with 2,000 kilos of force. And no one would have realized because it was hidden underneath her body, a heavy wooden plank and the grandeur of a grown elephant. Perhaps she would have tried to gasp or scream as the knife plunged in. And in order to scream she would have to let out her breath. If she let out her breath, the weight of the elephant would crush her body in an instant. She certainly would have died, if not from the stab wound then from the mass of the elephant, right before the eyes of a live audience.

This was not a mistake, an instance of a careless stagehand overlooking a pebble on the ground. *This was intentional.*

'Someone wanted to kill me.' Reba said out loud, perhaps to herself, perhaps to Ghosh, perhaps to no one.

They were both horrified. Silenced. Reba was afraid for her life, yet relieved she had lived. Someone wanted to murder her.

They slowly stepped back, the knife lying there under the lights of the ring. The mattress lay torn open. They faced the knife for several steps, then turned their backs to the scene and walked to the dressing area. There was nothing more that could be said. In stunned silence Reba gathered her things, not bothering to change out of her costume, and walked out into the Calcutta night air with Ghosh by her side. Together they rode north.

Working solely on muscle memory, Reba prepared herself for bed. Her mind, which had been racing during the act, was silent now. Not peaceful, but completely blank. She let the void of sleep overtake her.

Someone tried to finish me off…

'Circus Beauty Queen' Reba—Wearing a Crown of Thorns

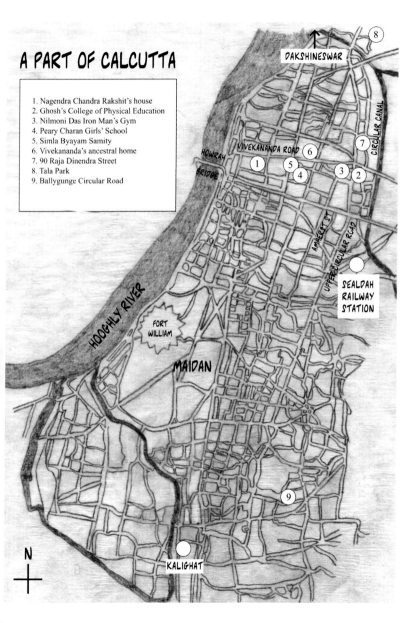

Drawn by Scott Lamps.

Reba Rakshit, circa 1950s.

Photo courtesy: *Swapan Talukdar. Further reproduction is prohibited without permission.*

Reba Rakshit with her elder sister Jyotsna.
Photo courtesy: *Swapan Talukdar. Further reproduction is prohibited without permission.*

Reba Rakshit in Full Lotus Pose.
Photo courtesy: *Swapan Talukdar. Further reproduction is prohibited without permission.*

Reba Rakshit graces the cover of *Byayam Charcha* magazine.

Photo courtesy: *Byayam Charcha*

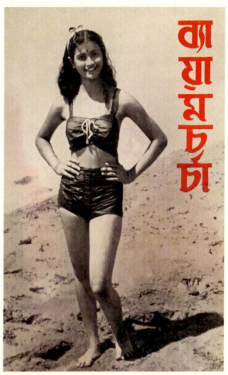

Signature of Reba Rakshit.
Photo by the author.

Reba Rakshit, circa 1950s.

Photo courtesy: *Byayam Charcha.*

Photo of Reba Rakshit's apartment at 90/1A Dinendra Street, Kolkata.

Photo taken by the author, 2019.

52A Ballygunge Circular Road, Kolkata. Reba Rakshit's apartment building where she lived later in her life.
Photo taken by the author, 2019.

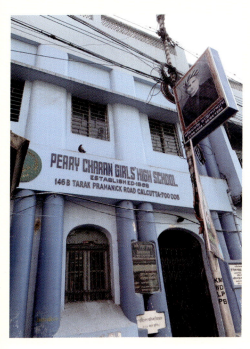

Peary Charan Girls' School, Kolkata.
Photo taken by the author, 2022.

'Anima Rakshit' listed in Peary Charan Girls' School registrar.

Photo courtesy: *Manimekhala Maiti. Photo taken by the author, 2022.*

Registrar of Peary Charan Girls' School 1928-1946.

Photo courtesy: *Manimekhala Maiti. Photo taken by the author, 2022.*

An advert by International Circus announcing amazing performances by artists, sportsmen and ferocious beasts. Miss Bengal, Miss India Reba Rakshit's exciting acts being the special attraction at Tala Park, Calcutta

Jugantar Vol: 24; Issue: 97 (25 December 1960) Accessed via the British Library Endangered Archives. Archives of the Centre for Studies in Social Sciences, Calcutta as custodian of digital copies.

Governor of West Bengal Kailash Nath Katju's letter in praise of the performance of Reba Rakshit.

Photo and document courtesy: *Romit Banerjee. Reproduction is prohibited without permission.*

I have had the pleasure of seeing the demonstrations of their skill and physical fitness by Master Dulal Kanji, Bengal Horizontal Bar and Tumbling champion as well as all-India Gymnastic champion. I have also seen with admiration the skill displayed by Kumari Labanya Palit and Kumari Reba Rakshit, Sri Gouri Shanker Mukherjee and Sri Bishnu Charan Ghosh in Sharp Shooting exercises. Physical fitness and endurance displayed by Kumari Labanya Palit in Motor Cycle jump demonstration was particularly striking. Sri Bishnu Charan Ghosh deserves encouragement and congratulations for the work he is doing in promoting the cause of physical fitness among the youth of Bengal.

Kailas Nath Katju

GOVERNMENT HOUSE,
DARJEELING,
31st May, 1950.

An advert by Bombay Circus announcing the unthinkable and impressive sports and skills of Miss Bengal 1955 Kumari Reba Rakshit for their evening show at Howrah Maidan

Jugantar Vol: 19; Issue: 65 (23 November 1955). Accessed via the British Library Endangered Archives. Archives of the Centre for Studies in Social Sciences, Calcutta as custodian of digital copies.

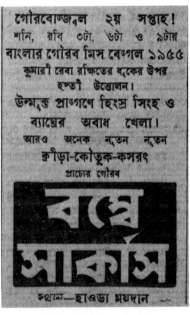

An advert announcing the glorious second week of Miss Bengal 1955 Kumari Reba Rakshit lifting an elephant on her chest. And many new sports, comedies and achievements including a free tiger and ferocious lion playing on the ground at Howrah Maidan.

Jugantar Vol: 19; Issue 75 (3 December 1955). Accessed via the British Library Endangered Archives. Archives of the Centre for Studies in Social Sciences, Calcutta as custodian of digital copies

Ghosh's College of Physical Education est. 1923.
Photo taken by the author.

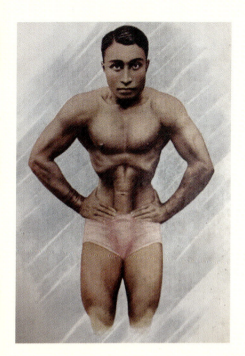

Bishnu Charan Ghosh—muscle control c. 1930.
Photo courtesy: *Ghosh Yoga College.*

Photo of the author with the original Bishnu Charan Ghosh's weights, thanks to Romit Banerjee.

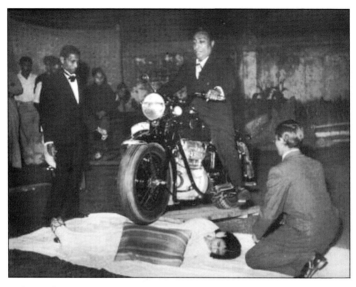

Reba performing the motorcycle stunt. Bishnu Charan Ghosh is riding the motorcycle, Gouri Shankar Mukerjee is kneeling.
Photo courtesy: *Romit Banerjee*.

Paramahansa Yogananda meditates. *Wikicommons*

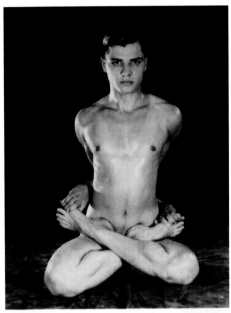

Buddha Bose in Bound Lotus Pose.
Photo courtesy: *Michael Shapiro*.

Labanya Palit in Lotus Pose
Photo courtesy: *The Centre for Studies in Social Sciences, Kolkata*.

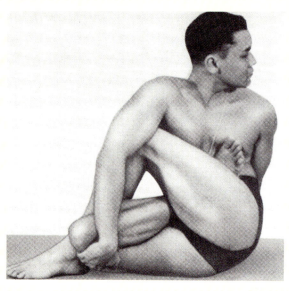

Gouri Shankar Mukerji in Full Spinal Twist Pose.
Photo courtesy: *Romit Banerjee*.

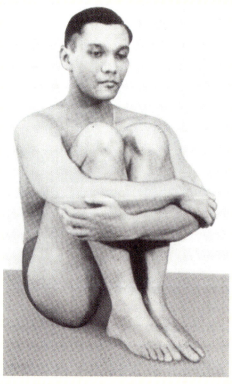

Gouri Shankar Mukerji in Seated Wind Removing Pose.
Photo courtesy: *Romit Banerjee*.

Sushila Sundari
Public domain.

Sushila Sundari with Shumbha and Nishumbha.
Public domain.

Bhabendra Mohan Saha with elephant on his chest.
Public domain.

Rama Murti Naidu 1930.
Public domain.

Bhim Bhabani.
Wikipedia.

Rama Murti Naidu.
Public domain.

17

Shows, Travel, Sleep

Did Reba Fully Belong to Herself?

As the winter faded and the circus season came to an end in Calcutta, so did Reba's contract. When the troupe packed up and left the city, she was not obligated to travel with them. But word about her incredible death-defying acts had spread far and wide and the circus owner was getting increasingly worried that if they showed up without Reba in the next city or the city after that, they would have to face either angry crowds or worse empty seats.

Reba was unsettled by the murder attempt on her life. No one knew who had planted the knife and there was no attempt to either discuss it or seek the truth. Everyone moved on. The show must go on.

There were times when trapeze artists fell, tiger acts went wrong; bones were broken and artists were replaced. Since Reba had walked away from the knife incident unharmed, she kept performing. She was *physically* capable of continuing. She was mentally capable too, but the constant fatigue of the act wore her down and an attempt on her life certainly did not help ease her predicament.

At the end of one evening's performance at the Maidan, the circus organizer approached Ghosh.

'Reba must sign on again and travel with the company,' he said, desperately trying to hide his anxiety under the confident tone.

'No, this is not possible!' Ghosh replied.

'She must come with us! Barasat, Bongaon, Basirhat ... News has already reached there! Reba is the star of the show!'

But Ghosh was firm.

'It is not possible. She won't go anywhere outside of Calcutta. I cannot make this request of her.'

'*Kono shomosha nei* (there is no problem). *Take jiggasha korbo* (I will ask her)!'

'OK, then. Ask her yourself. See if she agrees.'

Once Reba had finished changing out of her leotard, she draped her saree and walked out of her changing room. She was tired from the act and ready to relax for the night. As she began to walk towards Ghosh, she was approached by the circus owner.

'Sister, you must sign a new contract.'

Reba stood, hearing him out.

'You must agree,' he continued. 'We will never survive the disappointment of the audiences. If they get to hear that your act is not in the performance, the company will be ruined.'[193]

Reba was not sure whether she was simply too tired to put up a fight, or whether a part of her wanted to sign a new

---

[193] Rakshit, 'The Sport of Elephant Lifting', 253-264.

contract. Even though she was aware of the threats to her life from the act—and now from the murder attempt—she was unsure of what her life would be like without the performances filling her schedule. What would she do with her time? What would she be? As all these questions rose in her tired mind, she was in no shape to sort them out. It was easier just to move forward, swallowed by the momentum of success than to change course.

Whatever the reason, she agreed to another contract.

The relief of the circus owner was palpable.

'We'll arrange everything,' he said. 'You'll only need to travel short distances away from Calcutta. You won't regret it.'[194]

We'll see about that, she thought tiredly.

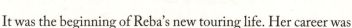

It was the beginning of Reba's new touring life. Her career was now in full swing. She was not just a performer in Calcutta. She was contracted to travel with the companies. She was the star of the show all around India.

Although the circus ran for only two months in Calcutta, the circus companies could not afford to run only two months a year, so the performers were contracted nearly year round. They simply had to move around to cater to demand under suitable conditions. So when demand waned in one city, the company just moved to another one.[195] This meant that Reba's life was now one for the road. She made her home in different cities for short bursts of time. However, when the circus

---

[194] Ibid.
[195] Ibid.

performed in cities reachable by train from Calcutta, she made the trip back and forth each day so that she could sleep in her own bed and maintain some pattern of a normal life.

Reba had moved out of her kaka's bari and into her own apartment at 90/1A Raja Dinendra Street. It was further from the Hooghly River and far to the east, in between Upper Circular Road and the canal. The house was only a ten-minute walk away from Ghosh's college. All she had to do to get to the gym was walk south on Raja Dinendra Street, past the ornately decorated buildings, cross the busy Vivekananda Road, turn right onto Rammohan Roy Road and she was at the alleyway which led to the college's tall metal gates.

Her new home was not too far from Sealdah railway station, which helped, now that she was travelling so much.[196] This station became the hub of her travel when the circus was performing in areas like Dum Dum, Barasat, Bongaon or Ranaghat. It was a hub for countless others as well. Reba arrived at the station in time for the afternoon train. She carried her suitcase which contained her evening's costume.

Now the station was crowded with people who lived there.[197] It still served as home to many who arrived around Partition. Train after train had pulled into Sealdah from the east. Many had come from Reba's homeland, but it was a home that now went by a new name, a different identity, a different meaning. Reba had to remember they had come from a place called East Pakistan. She was lucky to have escaped the mass upheaval of Partition and was fortunate to have a safe and comfortable home, a flourishing career and a family.

---

[196] Ibid.
[197] 'History of Sealdah Station', Indian Railway Rules, 23 June 2020. https://www.indianrailwayrules.com/history-of-sealdah-station/

Many arrived at Sealdah station during Partition only to be faced with the fact that there was no further place to go. The platforms remained crowded with Hindu refugees.[198] The ones who were literate, or had other resources, were easily able to occupy land and establish a new home. But those who were poor relied heavily on relief camps or government assistance. In the 1950s, sometimes as many as 5,000 refugees were living on Sealdah's twelve platforms. It was only in 1962, two years after Reba stopped travelling with the circus that the number of refugees at the station decreased.[199]

With only two latrines available for women, there were frequent outbreaks of cholera and smallpox. Despite the immense challenges, some took whatever opportunity they could get and opened up little shops selling rice, paan or cigarettes to the many travellers passing through. As Reba made her way to the train bound for Bongaon, she could not avoid the constant reminders of the conditions people were living in. It infiltrated her senses, sight and smell especially. As she took her seat on the train, Ghosh by her side, the afternoon sun streamed through the windows. The world spun around her.

She felt exhausted.

Her body was perpetually in a state of recovery. She would sleep what felt like endlessly, waking up in the morning with an intense cloudiness in her head and heaviness in her body. She had to sleep at least eight hours a night, but that left very

---

[198] Anwesha Sengupta, 'The Railway Refugees of Bengal Partition: Revisiting Sealdah Station of 1950s–60s', https://www.academia.edu/45600279/The_Railway_Refugees_of_Bengal_Partition_Revisiting_Sealdah_Station_of_1950s_60s
[199] Ibid.

little time for anything else. Shows, travel, sleep—the routine was constant; it did not let up.

Reba reflected on her school studies while the train crept northeast towards Bongaon. She had passed her intermediate exams and was planning to take the BA exam. After attaining success and fame, she found it increasingly hard to put her mind on her studies. She would either be preoccupied with her performance, or allow her mind to drift off and rest.

By late afternoon, Reba and Ghosh arrived in Bongaon. The circus that evening would feature trapeze acts, animal performances and Reba's many acts. She would perform five or six different stunts including weightlifting, sharpshooting, knife throwing and, of course, the elephant lift.[200] The newspapers were correct when they wrote:

Kumari Reba Rakshit
(courtesy of Bishnu Charan Ghosh)
Her incredible and impressive sportswomanship
will keep you enthralled from start to finish![201]

From start to finish, Reba stole the show. All of her acts required incredible skill and precision. Balancing a heavy barbell overhead with weights on either end required balance and stability. Balance was no problem for her, as she was diligently practising asanas and performing these postures sometimes as well. The stability necessary for weightlifting was a good complement to the bending and twisting the asanas

---

[200] Rakshit, 'The Sport of Elephant Lifting', 253-264.
[201] *Jugantar*, Vol.19, Issue 65 (23 November 1955), British Library, EAP262/1/2/19/325, https://eap.bl.uk/archive-file/EAP262-1-2-19-325

required. The elephant stunt was no doubt life-threatening, but the *easier* act of motorcycle lifting was perilous also. One error in judgement as to when to breathe, one incorrect flinch of a muscle and she could be dead. The dangers of the stunts, along with her ever-growing presence in the public's eye, not to mention her recent brush with death, made her feel as though she was constantly flirting with danger. She always tried to calm herself, thinking that her guru knew what he was doing and he always had an eye out for her. However, there was yet another stunt she performed that brought her to the fine line between skill and luck—the knife-throwing stunt.

The act of throwing a knife usually involves two people—the one who throws the knife and the one who serves as the target. But Reba's knife-throwing act was twice as complicated because she was *both* the thrower and the target.

She stood to the side of the ring with knives in hand. The crowd cheered wildly as they caught sight of Reba. Many had come just to see her. The music picked up energy, the emcee announced loudly, 'The pride of Bengal! Kumari Reba Rakshit!'

Reba entered wearing a white leotard and an elegant pair of white sandals with a little high heel. She walked confidently and elegantly. Her hair was pinned up neatly and tightly. For this stunt, nothing could be hanging loose from her body or waving in the wind. Nothing that she did not want shredded to pieces.

The crowd stayed lively as she acknowledged them. She waved the sharp blades of the knives in the air so they caught the light, displaying their power to pierce through anything.

Reba stood in the middle of the ring.

She looked up, focusing on where in the air the knives would swirl. She looked down to see exactly where she would position herself once the stunt began.

All the while, the crowd's eyes followed Reba. They were not exactly sure what she was about to do.

Then it all happened in a blink.

Reba threw two knives up high in the air. They swirled, handle over blade, again and again, the shiny silver metal catching the light as they travelled higher and higher.

The crowd looked up for a moment, watching the knives and then back down and at Reba.

With one swift and precise move, Reba dropped down onto the stage, lying flat on her back. The knives reached their pinnacle and started falling back towards Reba's body.

She held herself perfectly still.

The knives fell. The tip of the blades pierced the wooden stage so that the handles stood upright in the air for all to see. They landed just next to Reba's body, one on either side of her. Without perfect precision, the momentum of the sharp knives would ensure that they easily slice through Reba, just like a piece of meat. The crowd waited for a moment, looking for any sign of the stunt going wrong.

Finally, after a long moment of restless waiting, Reba got up from in between the knives. The crowd erupted in joy, releasing the tension of their fear and wonder. She bent over and pulled the knives out of the ground, tugging hard to dislodge their blades. She stood proudly, waved the shiny weapons in the air. She smiled and bowed. Then she walked off the stage just as elegantly as she had walked on.

Another success, she thought. *Now the elephant stunt.*

As soon as the show was over, Reba quickly left for the train station at Bongaon. She needed to catch the last train back to Sealdah. The station master at Bongaon knew Reba and made sure the train did not leave without her.

Furthermore, he made sure that a first-class compartment was kept reserved for her.

The dark sky hung over the station as Reba arrived. She crawled into her cabin, grateful for the reserved spot. Her eyes blurred for a moment. Her breath felt short, her chest a bit tight. A dull ache pulsed in her head. She started to drift in and out of sleep as the train chugged down the tracks towards Calcutta.

It was the middle of the night when the train finally pulled into Sealdah station in Calcutta. Reba gathered her things from her compartment and walked down the crowded platform. Many people were lying down side by side, asleep among the clatter of the trains on the tracks. She longed to be asleep and could feel how close she was to home. Finally when she reached the city, she quickly exited the station and walked straight to the car that was waiting for her. At this time of the night, the roads were quieter than they were in the afternoon when she left. Once she reached home, she simply crashed.

When she awoke, Reba realized she had a little blood crusted under her nose. *Another nose bleed.* They were happening more frequently now. She felt tired and longed to stay home for the day, but had to give in to the demands of her contract and the same routine—station, show, station, home.

Of course, it was not all aches and pains. The crowds were warm and she felt immense pleasure as she felt their admiration for her. The newspapers printed her name constantly, and the money she made from the circus was piling up. She was starting to feel like she should consider taking a break. She did not need more money and her body could use with some rest. She decided to forgo another contract if and when they offered it to her and instead focus on teaching yoga if she needed to earn some money. She deeply desired to stay at home and rest.

The shows at Bongaon were coming to an end, and Reba's contract was ending along with them. As Reba prepped herself for her last show, the circus manager entered her dressing area and announced, 'Next is Siliguri!'

Since Siliguri was nestled way up in north Bengal, Reba was not keen to travel that far, or start a new contract for that matter!

'Siliguri, then Katihar and Silchar,' he announced.

Reba simply could not believe what she was hearing. These were far, far away from home! Silchar was even further east than Comilla! If she signed the contract, she would never be home.

Reba informed him that she would not sign on for the shows.

'We will pay you more!' the manager said desperately.

Reba was only thinking of the travel involved, the pay was not on her mind at all.

'Five thousand for forty shows! For the weekend shows, we will pay even more!'

Reba still resisted.

When he first made the proposal, it did not strike Reba as noteworthy. Later, she did not have it in her to resist the offer.

Reba still resisted.

But as it was, she could only resist for so long since she was not in a position to fully determine her own fate. The circus companies put on such pressure consistently saying that they could not do it without her. Also, Ghosh needed her to continue. She was bringing fame and notoriety to his college, which badly required both in order to flourish. She was a star performer who simply did not fully belong to herself. She partially belonged to the audience who never had enough of her, the companies that promoted her and the person who trained her.

She signed on to perform in Siliguri and the cities that followed. She was venturing further and further from Calcutta. The pace of her life quickened with each success. Whenever she could, Reba made little requests that helped ease the demands of her schedule. If she was performing in a matinee show, she made sure her act was the last one. That way she had enough time to eat lunch and rest before performing. On the weekends, which generally had three shows on a day, she would perform after five or six acts in the six o'clock show, but perform third in the night show. That ensured she sleep quickly and easily, instead of waiting up late to perform.

Reba's contracts ran their course, but her routine kept on. The raging success of her performances kept her in public life. Except Calcutta, most of these performances were restricted in small cities in eastern India. Soon it would be time to test herself among some of the country's most famous and successful performers.

She was headed to Bombay.

18

Would Ghosh's Experiment Succeed?

Mastering the Art of Survival

As Reba's popularity grew, it was only a matter of time before she found herself in Bombay, the home of the Hindi film industry and the greatest celebrities in the country.

She landed in Bombay at the request of the owner of Gemini Circus, M.V. Sankaran—the pioneer of the modern Indian circus.[202]

As a boy, Sankaran was completely enthralled by the circus when it came to Kolaserry in Kerala. He started training in circus arts but soon ended up working in wireless communications for the military and served in the army during

---

[202] M.K. Sunil Kumar, 'Lord of the Rings', *The Times of India*, 2021, https://timesofindia.indiatimes.com/blogs/tracking-indian-communities/lord-of-the-rings/

World War II. After the war, he joined a *kalari* school where the circus performers would come and train. He was interested in the flying trapeze.

After performing for a few years, he along with his colleague invested in Vijaya Circus which had come up for sale. He later rebranded it according to his zodiac sign, Gemini.[203]

Sankaran had seen Reba perform with the Oriental Circus and was completely mesmerized by her act.[204] He could clearly see her immense talent, with her ability to do such a wide variety of acts. Her beauty, grace and unbelievable strength was compelling to watch. He was eager to hire talent that was well trained and could connect well with the audience in order to keep them coming back.

He signed Reba for a three-month contract in Bombay.

Bombay was a whole new world for Reba. It was bursting with talent, passion and extravagance. Massive crowds came to see the circus with more and more stars among them.

The circus tent was raised near Dadar Station. The tents were always raised on an auspicious time on an auspicious day, usually a Wednesday. The ceremony would also take place on a Monday or a Sunday, but never on a Tuesday or Saturday. A puja would take place in which coconuts and bananas were distributed as prasad. Kumkum was applied to the poles and camphor was burnt.[205] Before the opening Friday performance, there was another puja in which five

---

[203] Rahul Chandran, 'The Circus Won't Die', *Mint*, 2014, https://www.livemint.com/Leisure/BpXr0tSctfzMYbTh2twDJI/The-circus-wont-die.html

[204] M.V. Sankaran, interview by Chandrima Pal, 3 April 2019.

[205] Nisha, *Jumbos and Jumping Devils*, 167.

more coconuts were broken. Only then would the opening performance take place.

The circus was so popular that getting a ticket was tough. The newspapers read:

Stupendous Spectacle!

Greatest show in Asia, the sensation of the season, teeming with thrills, packed with excitement, is in town with superlative performances that have stunned spectators!

Crowds Throng at the Dadar Grounds And Many Have to Go Back for Want of Tickets … And Gemini offers apologies to them for their disappointment.

DON'T MISS TO MEET MISS INDIA 1957 REBA RAKSHIT, and don't lose the rare thrill of your lifetime as you witness an elephant walking over her chest! Every Man, Woman and Child is talking of the incomparable.[206]

By now, newspapers repeatedly claimed that Reba had been given prestigious awards for her skill and beauty, like 'Miss Bengal 1955' or 'Miss India 1957'. But the truth was, Reba was Miss Circus, if anything. Her whole life was the circus now, and she sacrificed her body to the performances every day. She probably did not need the embellished accolades but they were added in the newspapers nonetheless. The Miss India pageant had started in 1947 and its first winner was from Calcutta. The pageant ran sporadically until 1955, when

---

[206] Classified Ad 3 – No Title. (6 November 1957). *The Times of India* (1861-2010). Accessed via British Library.

it stopped for a few years before resuming in 1959. So it was convenient to call Reba the winner of 1957 since there was no official winner to speak of. Perhaps it was also on many people's minds as the film *Miss India* came out the same year as her alleged title. Marketing strategies, Ghosh's included, were fond of hyperbolic statements of greatness, whether or not they represented reality.

Many of the early winners of the pageant were now film stars. On any given night, many popular stars in the movie business were in the audience. After the show when they would come to greet Reba, she felt like she was meeting her heroes over and over again. She shook their hands and marvelled at the strange course her life had taken. They complimented her on her incredible abilities: 'We just act in front of a camera, where it is perfectly safe,' they said. 'There is no danger in our work that we will be stabbed or crushed.'

David, best known for his portrayal of John Chacha in *Boot Polish*, was the one Reba was overwhelmed to meet. He was an incredibly popular actor who had already been recognized by the Filmfare Awards. Apart from acting in an impressive number of films, he was a sporting enthusiast. Like Reba, he was interested in not only performance but also athletics.

Mala Sinha was another. Reba could relate to her as they both hailed from Bengal, they both performed in order to entertain their audience and they were both pushing the boundaries of what it meant to be a woman performer. They had both become famous with all the wealth and infamy that it brought.

Then another of her heroes came to watch her perform—Raj Kapoor.

For Raj Kapoor, cinema was everything. There was a world beyond cinema, but it mattered only because it could be brought into film. So, when Raj Kapoor saw Reba perform with Gemini Circus, his reaction was not one of simple appreciation rather it came with the idea that *she* should be brought into one of his films. If the circus was impressive in real life, it would be even more wonderful when depicted on the big screen. He insisted that Reba join him and star in one of his movies.

However, Suhasini was not amused by the idea of Reba starring in one of Raj Kapoor's films. Whether it was her mother's request or the reality of her demanding contract, Reba did not take up the opportunity. Eventually though, she did appear in the 1958 film *Great Show of India* since it had the circus as a backdrop to themes of romance, quarrels, jealousy and heartache. Kamini Kaushal and Mahipal were the leads in it. The newspapers did not fail to mention that 'the circus beauty queen, Reba Rakshit and other circus artists perform in this thrilling picture'.[207]

Despite the constant attention from film stars and political figures like Bombay's mayor or the founding member of the Communist Party of India (CPI), S. A. Dange, Reba was eager to return to Calcutta and live a more normal life.

The stage life was wearing on her—the brute physical effort to carry herself to show after show; the immense toll the acts took on her; and all of the running around from city to city. She never had time to develop relationships or settle into a routine at home and live a normal life. In Bombay, she

---

[207] 'Great Show of India Opens Today.' 'Chandan' enters third week. (9 May 1958). *The Times of India (1861–2010)*. Accessed via British Library.

was a stranger, so far from home, which made her feel even more unsettled. The reality settling in her heart made her feel like a stranger in her own mind. She now felt she was playing the part of Reba the circus star, questioning who she really was anymore.

Even when Reba was done in Bombay, her contracts with Gemini Circus were still in full swing. The troupe finished a run of shows in Jamalpur in Bihar. Their next show was in Asansol with four days of rest in between. It was then Reba decided to go home for a break.[208]

As they headed home for Calcutta, Ghosh caught a glimpse of Reba's eyes and suddenly said, 'Look at me! Let me see! Why is there blood in your eyes?'[209]

Reba had not felt anything out of the ordinary but upon a closer look, they realized her eyes were bloodshot.

Ghosh looked worried, unlike his usual stoic self. His mouth turned downwards in a tight frown as he looked into the distance, clearly thinking hard. He was anxious.

'Once we reach Calcutta, we will go immediately to the doctor,' he said finally.

Dr Nihar Munsi was a legendary eye doctor.[210] His service to the community as well as his exceptional accuracy in eye surgery made him a household name. Shortly after reaching Calcutta, Ghosh and Reba went to consult Dr Munsi at Hazra Road.

On examination of Reba's eyes, the doctor was deeply concerned. Her condition was serious. Blood would need to be extracted from Reba's eye using a syringe, which was a delicate and risky procedure.

---

[208] Rakshit, 'The Sport of Elephant Lifting', 253-264.
[209] Ibid.
[210] https://nmefkolkata.com

'I will not be able to perform this right now,' he informed Reba. But one thing had to happen immediately. 'You must stop elephant lifting once and for all.'[211]

Reba was distraught because of her prior commitments.

'Inform them that I'm not available,' she dejectedly mumbled to her Bishtuda.

Ghosh felt that the circus company would not believe them. Reba was too big a star. They would need to see her condition, to really see the blood clot in her eyes, to understand that she could not withstand the pressure of elephants any longer.

'We'll go and inform them. Let them see you,' Ghosh replied.

Reba's mind was in a turmoil. She was deeply disappointed and extremely fearful of losing her eyesight or worse. As she processed the turn of events, all of her thoughts slowly merged into a stunned, flat feeling.

Her guru interrupted her introspection.

'We'll get the medical certificate and show them.'

Like always, her Bishtuda had decided on a course of action. Reba went along with it.

They arrived in Asansol. But the medical certificate could not convince the owner that she would not perform. She could hear Ghosh trying to interject, but falling short of the owner's demands.

'Nonsense!' the circus man yelled angrily, waving his arms in the air and pointing to the seats that would soon be filled with paying spectators. 'The audience will burn the whole camp down if Reba Rakshit's event is missing!'

---

[211] Rakshit, 'The Sport of Elephant Lifting', 253-264.

As Reba listened, she thought about the contract she had signed and the pact she had made. The respect and care she received, the money, the fame, it all came at a price. She was the princess of Gemini Circus. Almost every newspaper of the day sang her praises.

> 'Her feat of bearing the weight of a huge elephant on her chest draws thundering applause from the audience!'[212]
>
> Or
>
> 'The show is packed with thrills, among the star performers being Reba Rakshit, winner of a physical culture and beauty award.'[213]
>
> Or
>
> 'Reba Rakshit — don't lose the rare thrill of your life-time as you witness an Elephant walking over her chest! Every Man, Woman and Child is talking of the incomparable Gemini Circus.'[214]

She *was* the circus. Sure there were other acts like the boneless act of Sheila, the fourteen-year-old 'Plastic Girl',[215] or a well-trained menagerie, comprising elephants, lions, tigers, horses,

---

[212] Gemini Circus Moves to Marine Drive. Classified ad 16 – no title. (20 November 1957). *The Times of India (1861–2010)*. Accessed via British Library.

[213] Gemini Circus By A Staff Reporter. Call to Follow Vegetarianism. (1957, Oct 13). *The Times of India* (1861-2010). Accessed via British Library.

[214] Classified ad 18 — no title. (1957, Nov 01). *The Times of India* (1861-2010). Accessed via British Library.

[215] Gemini Circus In Town. (21 December 1962). *The Times of India (1861-2010)*. Accessed via British Library.

zebras, etc., and a host of skilful Indian and foreign artists.[216] But the Gemini Circus was 'the Gem of a Circus' and the star act was 'Miss Reba Rakshit's astounding feat of bearing the burden of an elephant on her chest'.[217] So, Ghosh decided to do an experiment.[218]

As the night fell, one by one the acts took to the stage. Reba watched as the animals danced, the plastic bodies bent and twisted, the jugglers bounced their objects in the air. Soon it was her turn.

The crowds were thundering in their anticipation but Reba's mind was silent. Yet again, her life was turned over to a higher power.

Would Ghosh's experiment succeed?

She tried to keep her mind placid as she went about the act, which was habitual by now.

Lie down.

Breathe in.

Hold.

Wait.

Thud, thud, thud, thud.

Exhale.

Applause.

Reba focused on the normal pattern of the act, visualizing the performance. It was Ghosh who adjusted the routine.

Grabbing a thin white rag, Ghosh knelt down by Reba's

---

[216] Gemini Circus. (9 December 1960). *The Times of India (1861–2010)*. Accessed via British Library.

[217] Gemini Circus Gala Opening To-Day. Classified Ad 21 – no title. (1957, Oct 17). *The Times of India (1861–2010)*. Accessed via British Library.

[218] Rakshit, 'The Sport of Elephant Lifting', 253-264.

head. He took the ends of the rag in both hands and scooped up the back of her head. He wrapped it around her head from front to back, pulling the fabric taught. He grabbed either end of the rag, making sure it was not bunched up or caught underneath her hair. Then he brought the ends of the fabric up over her forehead. Creasing and twisting, he knotted the fabric on her forehead just above her eyes. Then, with his own muscles rippling underneath his black suit, he pulled in either direction, securing the knot as tightly as he could like a tourniquet.

It squeezed Reba's head intensely.

The idea was to control and limit the pressure on the brain. But of course the fabric was tied *outside* of her skull and the blood pressure *in* her skull was the area of concern. In actuality, the fabric could not do anything about the pressure no matter how tightly it was pulled. But if it made Ghosh feel better about the risk, perhaps it did its job.

Once the fabric was drawn tight, Ghosh took a seat at Reba's head. He folded his legs, her head resting by his ankles. The heavy wooden plank was draped upon her chest as though it were a silk scarf. Perhaps the crowd would recognize the wooden plank as an effortless though necessary part of the act. Reba knew the difference. The plank alone weighed more than she did. While she was used to it, she was not used to the veins in her head being on the verge of bursting. *Would the blood seep from her eyes? Would her veins burst, drowning her brain?* A brief moment of consideration washed through her, before the silence returned.

The stillness.

The acceptance.

Or was it just the blank feeling that happens when *feeling* is just too much to handle?

Ghosh, sitting with his legs crossed, bent slightly forward and placed his thumbs near her temples.[219] As the elephant began to step onto Reba's chest, Ghosh strongly pressed just in the space where her veins typically darkened as they bulged out of her fair skin. This time they stayed thin, or at least it seemed so as they were covered under Ghosh's wide thumbs. His dark brown eyes stayed like a laser at Reba, monitoring her for anything out of the ordinary.

Reba stayed in her silent, wordless state.

As the elephant stepped off her, the pressure ceasing, Ghosh removed his thumbs from her temples, slowly moving his hands to the sides, waiting for any sudden change in her delicate condition.

Then just as always, the plank was removed. The stagehands vigorously rubbed her limbs and cheeks. They pulled her to her feet.

Reba stood. Her veins had not torn open, there was no sign of blood clotting in her eyes.[220]

She stood to a crowd erupting in awe, but their applause was no match for the silence still overwhelming her. Hazy, distant images surrounded her in all directions. She was in both a clear state of presence and a dull impenetrable state. As though she had stepped out of herself, she was aware she was acknowledging the crowd, basking in their admiration. Still dazed, she pulled the cloth from her forehead and adjusted her leotard. The stark, blankness of the moment seemed to carry

---

[219] Ibid.
[220] Ibid.

on into infinity. The slow-motion haziness of the evening floated around her.

As she turned to walk out of the ring, a singular thought rang through her mind. It penetrated her entire being as it boomed clearly in her mind, heart and body, all at the same moment. With each step she took out of the ring, the syllables of her thoughts unfolded with such great clarity. As she stepped out of the ring, the thought grew louder: *I cannot keep this up much longer.*

19

Circus, Yoga and Magic—Intertwined Together

Reba at the P.C. Sorcar Show

Reba did not renew her contract with Gemini Circus and returned to Calcutta. She had been far from home for so long, far from her parents, uncle, sister and nephew. Even though she was constantly surrounded by adoring fans and celebrities, she often felt lonely. Her stardom and money kept growing, but so did the things she missed. She was ready to have a more ordinary life. To her, an ordinary life was something rare, something special, something extraordinary.

In the autumn months, Calcutta was busy with festivities surrounding Vishvakarma Puja, Durga Puja, Kali Puja and Diwali.

Reba was happy to be home for the pujas. As the city slowed down and people stopped working for a few days, the atmosphere was relaxed and happier. The hectic energy of the streets became almost peaceful, almost serene. In the days leading up to the puja, people were neck-deep shopping new clothes for themselves and their loved ones. It was a time of abundance and joyful celebration.

As Durga Puja approached, spectacular pandals were built in almost every neighbourhood, partially blocking the alleyways.

As Reba stood in front of Durga Ma in her neighbourhood pandal, she thought *We must overcome evil. It is never easy; it is always changing shape and attacking from another side. But we must persevere and good will triumph. I wonder if Ma Durga stepped on Mahishasura's chest, will he be crushed? He probably doesn't know how to hold his breath. I wonder if I could survive. Probably not!*

Reba was peaceful and happy. After so many months of non-stop hard work and travel, it felt good to stand for a moment in the warm darkness of the Calcutta night admiring representations of beauty, love and goodness.

That autumn, Ghosh asked Reba to perform a stunt for Vishvakarma Puja. Hers would be the opening act for the world-famous Bengali magician P. C. Sorcar.

'It will be simple,' Ghosh said. 'Just lift a motorcycle. It will not be a problem. And you will share the stage with one of the greatest performers alive!'

Reba could not say no.

The circus, yoga and magic were closely related in India. They all involved elements of performance and mysticism, so it was not surprising when their worlds intertwined.

Indian magicians were portrayed as mystics or fakirs with supernatural abilities. The Great Indian Levitation Trick or the Basket Trick or the Mango Tree Trick have kept the masses entertained and intrigued for ages.

The trick was legendary and accounts of Bengali jugglers performing this act date back to the early 1600s. With the advent of the twentieth century, the attitude towards Indian magicians started to change, much as the view of Indians was changing in other fields like bodybuilding and yoga. What had been a largely demeaning view portraying them as inferior started to shift course. In the twentieth century, the Western fascination with 'the Orient' grew. Around the mid-twentieth century, Indian magicians used television shows to create notoriety much faster among many more viewers in one setting. A perfect example of this was P. C. Sorcar.

P. C. Sorcar, born near Dacca not very far from Comilla, was masterful at the art of illusion and creating new magic tricks. He was also a sharp businessman and used newspapers, pamphlets, radio, television and a journal, the All India Magic Circle, to promote himself far and wide. When performing in London, he walked around with an entourage of women dressed in sarees, capitalizing on what was clearly an unusual sight to the average Londoner. P. C. Sorcar was extremely innovative, both in his performances and in his marketing, and incredibly hard-working.[221] He performed across the world. And it was in Calcutta that he performed with Reba as his opening act.

Huge crowds gathered at the Vishvakarma Puja organized by Usha Engineering Company. Since the puja is in homage to building and construction skills, those who worship Vishvakarma often do so in their place of work, in front of their tools, rather than in a temple.

---

[221] Sarah Dadswell, 'Jugglers, Fakirs, and Jaduwallahs: Indian Magicians and the British Stage', *New Theatre Quarterly*, 23, Issue 1 (2007), 3–24.

In the time of creation, the Creator was imagined as a sculptor, a smith, a woodcutter, a carpenter.[222] The hymns of creation imagine the world carved out of a great block of wood. The hymns ask:

> What was the base, what sort of raw matter was there, and precisely how was it done, when the All-Maker, casting his eye on all, created the earth and revealed the sky in its glory?
>
> What was the wood and what was the tree from which they carved the sky and the earth? You deep thinkers, ask yourselves in your own hearts, what base did he stand on when he set up the worlds?[223]

Today there are only a few temples that stand in Vishvakarma's honour alone. But he appears in Vaishnava temples, often pictured as a man with a white beard and tools in his left hand. He is thought to be the sculptor who created the Jagannath Temple in Puri. But Vishvakarma had another side too. He used sacrifice as offering:

> Those forms of yours that are the highest, those that are lowest, and those that are in the middle, O All-Maker, help your friends to recognize them in the oblation. You who follow your own laws, sacrifice your body yourself, making it grow great.[224]

---

[222] Wendy Doniger O'Flaherty, *The Rig Veda: An Anthology* (New Delhi: Penguin Books, 2000), 34–35.
[223] *Rg Veda* 10.81.4, ibid., 35.
[224] Ibid.

Reba and Ghosh stood to the side of the small stage which was arranged in front of the Usha Engineering Company pandal. Tens of thousands crowded in the street around the pandal to pay their respects and see the performances. The people were packed shoulder to shoulder so there was no room for a large performance ring, only the small stage.

But Reba was worried. This arrangement was quite different from the circus, where the audience was seated in their own section and the performers had plenty of space to execute their dangerous acts. She was not sure that there was enough room here for the motorcycle to approach and drive over her safely.

There is nothing that can be done, she thought. It was here that Reba would have to perform the motorcycle stunt and warm up the audience for the great P.C. Sorcar. [225]

As they waited for the motorcycle to arrive, Reba turned to her Bishtuda and said, 'I have a bad feeling about this,' she said. 'The space is too small to perform.' Reba did not want this to go badly and create a situation where *she* would become the sacrifice.

But Ghosh assured her, 'Don't worry. It's my responsibility.'[226]

Reba wondered whether he meant it was his responsibility to protect her, or to ensure that the show was a success. Sometimes she wondered if he got swept away in the performance so much that he was willing to *hope* for the best in regard to her safety. Would he rely on Vishvakarma's *creation* so much that he would forget about *sacrifice*? The Rig Veda hymn says: 'You who follow your own laws, sacrifice your body yourself, making it grow great.'[227]

---
[225] Rakshit, 'The Sport of Elephant Lifting', 253-264.
[226] Ibid.
[227] O'Flaherty, *The Rig Veda: An Anthology*.

Finally, Pravas arrived with a particularly impressive motorcycle. It was heavy, with thick, broad tires. Ghosh would stand guard, instructing each moment, Prabhas would drive and Reba would lie underneath the motorcycle. This was supposed to be the act, to be performed before a crowd of nearly 50,000 people looking on.

It was not only Reba who was in a precarious position. The motorcycle had to accelerate quickly to pick up enough speed to hit Reba's chest with the force required to take flight. By the time it reached Reba, the motorcycle was travelling fast. It was almost impossible to stop or change direction. So, the approach left no room for error. That day, it would have to navigate a crowd which was packed like sardines.

Reba wondered why this thought did not seem to cross the minds of those watching the performance. Then she realized. *Of course. It is always better to get in on the action than to miss out.* She scrambled over to Pravas who was tugging at his suit coat, straightening out wrinkles from the ride over.

'Pravasda, what is going to happen today?'

Her voice was anxious, the tone higher than usual.

'I don't know anything, talk to Bishtuda.'

She was annoyed at his dismissive attitude. Just at that moment, Ghosh came with instructions.

'Reba, lie down.'

His command was direct and unwavering.

She obeyed. Still anxious, she knelt down and then rolled onto her back. Once down, something uncomfortable pressed back against her head. Almost a poking feeling, but strong like a brick. She turned her head to alleviate the pain. But just as she did, Ghosh corrected her, calling out in his thunderous way.

'Why are you turning your head?! The camera won't catch your face!'

Besides the thousands who would watch the event live, the whole performance was going to be captured on film.

Reba did not really care if her face was on camera, in fact, she hoped it would not be, though that was not the reason she turned her head. She responded, 'It is hurting, there's something there!'

All her trepidation about the event was putting her mind in the land of *what ifs*. *What if something goes wrong? What if, instead of the stunt succeeding, my head is smashed to pieces? Or my brain explodes in all directions like a dropped melon?*

'Why are you turning your head?' Ghosh asked yet again.

'I don't care if the camera won't catch my face!'

So much for Ghosh's resolve. Today, Reba got her way.

It was a good thing. Reba's hunch that something might go wrong was nearly proven right. The turn of her head to the side was the difference between life and death.

Pravas revved up the engine. Smoke puffed out from the back of the bike. The crowd's excitement grew.

Lying down, Reba could see everything. In the last few moments before the stunt her anxiety grew.

The crowd is too close, she thought. *There isn't enough room to do this right.*

Then Pravas accelerated to the crowd's roaring cheers.

The angle of his approach was not quite right. Pravas had to manoeuvre slightly to avoid the crowd, which meant that he had to adjust at the last moment in order to go up the plank and over Reba.

He did not quite make it.

The first tyre made contact with Reba's body.

Then came the second.

The hind tyre of the motorcycle skidded across the side of Reba's face.

Then her world went black.

The crowd collectively gasped but Reba did not hear it. All that she knew at that moment was complete darkness.

Reba's memory of the moments that followed were only shades of grey. Not even the thundering roar of the crowd could revive her. Not even Pravas and Ghosh scooping her limp body up in their arms and carrying her away from the spectators.

She was out cold.

Back behind the pandal, she lay still for quite some time. In the darkness, her head began to radiate sharp, splintering pain.

She registered the pain.

I can feel something. I'm alive.

As she slowly became conscious of her thoughts again, Reba wondered what the audience must have thought. They would surely think she was dead.

I am not dead, though.

I am aware.

I am alive.

As she tried to think about the crowd and what exactly they had just witnessed, the thoughts were too much for her foggy mind. Instead, she carefully propped herself on her elbows, trying to sit up.

Slowly, slowly.

She looked down at her dress, dirt and oil from the motorcycle tainted the fabric.

Another damaged dress, she thought.

Letting out a tiny grunt, she sat all the way up, her head

throbbing with each movement. Then she caught a glimpse of herself in the reflection of Pravas's rear-view mirror. Her dark hair was matted, some of it stuck to her face. As she brought her hand up to her cheek, she tried to pull her hair back to her ear. Instead of just her hair, she felt thick, hot sticky goo. She pulled her hand back down and stared at her fingers. They were black. Covered in a gluey rubber. She looked back towards the motorcycle now parked next to her. She leaned in slightly, into her reflection in the motorcycle's fender. She turned her chin to the left, just as she had done in the stunt.

There it was. The dark black tread of the tire, stained into her cheek.

It was as if sculpted into her skin, like a tattoo scorched the imprint deep into her face. Reba lay back down slowly, the headache still clouding her thoughts. She was conscious now but resorted back to darkness, the trauma of the day running its course.[228]

For months she scrubbed her face, trying to remove the injured spot.

---

[228] Ibid.

20

The Final Bow

Reba Sets the Barbell Down

In 1960, Reba started a new contract with the International Circus. Despite its name, this was the local one and she liked the hometown feel of it. She felt she had another contract in her, so long as she did not have to travel and be away from home. Plus, in this show she could diversify her acts. In Bombay, she had almost exclusively done what she was known for—the elephant stunt. But now she could bring back bodybuilding and other supplemental performances. These were not as hard on her body and after the show she could sleep in her own apartment.

The Calcutta newspapers printed photos and big advertisements presenting Reba as the main attraction:

International Circus
Under the direction of Byayamacharya Sri Bishnu Charan Ghosh, Reba Rakshit's exciting performance![229]

As always, Reba kept a busy schedule. The performances ran three times a day, at 2 p.m., 5 p.m. and 8 p.m. They were held north of the canal at Tala Park in north Calcutta.

She was glad to be back home and not so removed from her neighbourhood and family. Travelling north each day, just beyond Shyambazar, was not bad considering all the years travelling outside the city on a daily basis.

Each day that she performed, the thought she could keep performing was overtaken by a truth building inside of her. It was growing in size from the tiny seed she had first felt in Bombay. This truth was rooting itself deep in her.

She really was nearing the end of her career.

Even though the papers continued to print her name and her picture, this truth would blossom at any moment. When it did, she knew what it would mean: whatever was next for her, it would not be this.

It was also time for the next generation. Audiences liked new acts, fresh talents and new faces. Ghosh did as well. He sculpted his prodigies into immense successes, but part of his craft was just that. He had to carve out new talent, spot new possibilities, make new worlds appear. His loyalty to his students ran deep, but the river of life flowed onwards, stopping for no one.

At home, Reba woke and immediately sat down on her cushion. In the comfort of her own space, she recognized

---
[229] *Jugantar*, Vol. 24 Issue 97 (25 December 1960), British Library, EAP262/1/2/24/297, https://eap.bl.uk/archive-file/EAP262-1-2-24-297

today felt different. Still groggy from sleep, she folded her legs in and stretched her spine upright. Sitting tall, she closed her eyes. She touched her left thumb and index finger together and rested her hand on her knee. She brought her right hand up to her face. With her thumb she closed her right nostril and took a deep and slow breath in through her left nostril. Then she closed her left nostril, opened her right and exhaled. As she inhaled again, this time through her right nostril, she slowed her breath down and began to feel herself settle. As she exhaled from the left nostril, she felt the sides of her body, not her physical body but something deeper, become balanced. Continuing to breathe in this pattern, she became increasingly alert, yet calm. Aware but relaxed.

After she finished her practice of *Anuloma Viloma Pranayama,* she mentally readied herself to go out in the world. From the quiet of her own space, she knew today was different. She could sense it.

Reba dressed for the first afternoon performance of the day at Tala Park. She stepped into her costume and pulled it up high, pulling her arms through the straps one by one. The bottom of the fabric rested high up on her thighs. She secured a black belt tightly around her waist, then pressed the V of the neckline flat down against her chest.

She had vast experience as a performer; she knew the routine without thinking. It was the same as it had always been: get ready, perform, get ready for the next show, perform. An endless cycle.

While her actions were the same, she felt reflective. Something was different now. Her body had borne the brunt of so much. The headaches, the soreness, the hectic travel life that left her exhausted. She had managed to make it to this point with not much more than the rubber markings etched on her face or the occasional blood clot in her eye. Considering she could have been crushed at any given moment by an elephant—or by the stress of success—she had managed a feat few could even imagine. She was still standing tall, still commanding the stage, still the star. In her there was the little girl who had always loved adventure, nature, daring feats and charting her own path. In her was also the woman she had become. Stepping into a new point in her life, her direction was bound to change.

The International Circus accommodated a smaller audience and was more intimate though no less enthusiastic.

As Reba walked into the centre of the ring amidst the roar of the crowd, a quietness filled Reba.

A barbell was resting on the ground with giant round weights on either end. Slowly, she bent over and wrapped her fingers around the metal. Her thumbs curled down and around the barbell. *Tight grip.* Then she picked it up, lifting it up to her thighs. As she did, the back of her body felt strong; the back of her legs powerful and stable, and her back strong and firm, holding her upright.

The crowd blurred …

She bent both of her knees slightly, giving herself the chance for a bit of power. Then in one swift moment, she pulled the bar up to her chest, straightening her knees and popping up onto her toes. She whipped her elbows forward away from her, underneath the bar, balancing it up by her shoulders. She waited there. The world around her murmured its admiration while holding still in anticipation for the beauty-queen-strong-woman's next move.

She stood. Then, in what appeared effortless, she popped the barbell up over her head, locking her elbows so that her arms were perfectly straight. She stood underneath the barbell, her left leg slightly forward and her right leg back for balance, toes turning out. She felt as though she was holding up the weight of the world. In some ways, she was.

She was always supporting something: the elephants, the weights, the circus company, the audience's admiration, her family, her guru. She had always delivered on her word—to be the great student, the great strong woman, the great star of the stage.

As she stood underneath the barbell, her vision became clear again. It had blurred from the blood clotting in her eye, the tyre marks on her face, and the wear and tear of the demanding performance schedule. Now as she looked around at the crowd, saluting them in her heart, she saw things clearly. She was not just saluting those present, but all the audiences she had ever performed for.

As her ears began to take in the noise, she heard the cheers ripple through the air in slow motion. She heard the gasps and applause.

To know the sound of something is to understand it, she thought. This yogic teaching resonated in her at that moment. To her the sound of the audience was to know what it was like to perform, to live the life she had been living, to be the person she was for so many.

Then her senses were drawn inwards once again. She had to be someone for so many. She was someone for her Bishtuda, a devoted talent who commanded the stage for years. Lately though, he was focused on developing his next batch of students. His younger children Bishwanath and Karuna were training under him to take over in the performance rings. Whether or not it was Reba at the centre, he was still chasing fame and glory. Japan was on his mind as he hoped to expand outside of India.

She was a *star* to other stars, actors, politicians, maharajas. She was an icon, a selling point, a spectacle to watch and admire. She was a sister, an aunty.

But perhaps there was more for her to be. Perhaps a teacher, a neighbour, a friend, perhaps even a mother and wife. Perhaps a new version of herself.

With the weight of the barbell overhead, she felt how much she had held up for so long. With every elephant she had carried, she had also held all the personas and the expectations. She had withstood every demand.

She was tired.

As she lowered the barbell back down to her chest, something flickered inside her. That heavy feeling she carried around was not just the weight of the stunts. It was the weight of knowing that things were changing. Now it was time to set down all the things she had been carrying for good. This phase of her life was over.

She dropped the barbell back down to her thighs.

Then she bent her knees, leaning over slightly.

As she set the barbell back down, the round plates touching the ground, she knew she was no longer carrying the weight of any of this.

I'm done.

Epilogue

Present Day

'Come!'

Ritu, the oldest of the girls, whispered to the others. They were gathering in the back room of the family home. The house was filled with their parents, seated on the bed and chairs, sipping tea. There was just enough conversation filling the room that the girls could slip away unnoticed.

Underneath the whirling fan spinning at a frantic speed, the girls began carefully gathering every pillow, every cushion, every cloth, every blanket around and stacking them one on top of another.

'We have another cushion at my home. I'll be right back,' said Dia, one of the younger girls. Careful tiptoes turned to a full-out dash once the little girl was out of her parents' sight. Quickly she ran, long and skinny limbs carrying her outside through the hot, stuffy air. She reached her home, went inside, and grabbed the gold-and-red cushion. Carefully, she lifted her dress and stuffed it as far up under the fabric as she could.

No one will notice, she thought.

Then Dia dashed back to her friends, this time clutching her belly to hold the cushion as her feet skipped over the tile floor.

As she reached the neighbour's home, she slowed her gait just in time to enter her parents' view. Just as she suspected, they did not bat an eye, but carried on with their neighbourhood gossip, not noticing her.

Entering the back room, she exclaimed in a high-pitched voice, 'I got it!'

With that, she lifted her dress once again, just enough for the pillow to plop out onto the ground. Then, standing as high on her tiptoes as she could, she pressed the cushion over her head, placing it on the top of the stack.

The girls giggled in excitement as they looked at the pile of pillows and blankets. It was a mountain, an Everest!

'Who is first?' Ritu asked, taking charge once again. The little one sat quiet, still catching her breath from her dash to retrieve the cushion.

Anaya, in a high-pitched but small voice, cried out, '*Ami ami* (I, I!)!'

The older girls were used to taking care of the little ones. Anaya and Dia were no longer babies, but were not yet old enough to fend for themselves. Ritu and her cousin Jaya often had to help their moms with work throughout the day. With their brothers away at school they would cut potatoes, wash the clothes, all the while keeping an eye on the little ones. Their love for their little sisters was sincere. Yet, in this instance it was not just their politeness that was willing them to let the little one go first. It was also their lack of confidence in what they were about to do. Better to let the little one try it first.

'Ok then, lie down,' Ritu said. Next to the giant stack of pillows, Anaya lay down flat on the solid and cool floor. Before she could straighten her dress, the others began.

'We'll just start with a few cushions.'

Carefully the girls started placing the pillows and cushions on top of Anaya. Anaya twitched a bit as the stack titled off balance.

'Be still! Don't move!' Ritu instructed.

Their giggles had turned silent. This was now a serious matter.

They continued stacking and stacking, higher than they could reach on their own. Pulling a stool near, they climbed up on the wood to stack the pillows even higher. With each new cushion, the weight increased on Anaya's chest.

'Okay, down there?' Jaya asked.

A muffled squeak of acknowledgement came out from down below.

'Now, hold your breath!'

To the others, Jaya shouted, '*Tin, Dui, Ek* ... (*3, 2, 1* ...)'

And with the countdown reaching its end, the girls themselves climbed on top of the pile. For a moment, they were so pleased with their ascent. They basked in their epic creation.

But just then a thought flashed through their minds.

We've got to get her out from underneath!

Frantically the girls jumped back to their feet, sliding off the edges of the pile. Then they dug to the bottom, throwing each pillow over their shoulders. They looked like animals digging frenetically, but with pillows and blankets instead of soil spraying into the air. Once they pulled the last pillow off Anaya's chest, they gathered around her.

'Shake her! We have to shake her arms and legs. That's what they do after the elephant stunt.'

Ritu instructed the others to do just what she had seen at the circus. They jiggled Anaya's arms and legs. Patted her cheeks and forehead.

With that, Anaya sprang up, her tiny feet catching the ground beneath her. Her dress wrinkled and hair standing on end from the friction and static electricity.

'Are you all right?' the girls cried out in unison, a hint of terror in their voices.

Standing proud and a bit taller than before, Anaya cried out, 'I did it! I'm strong just like Reba!'

A seed of strength had been planted in every Bengali girl's heart. It was matched only by a seed of courage.

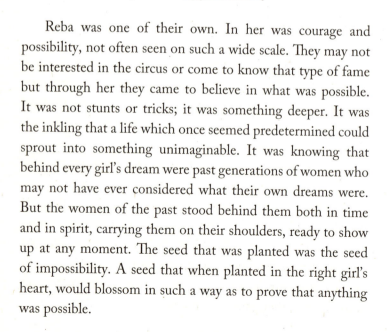

Reba was one of their own. In her was courage and possibility, not often seen on such a wide scale. They may not be interested in the circus or come to know that type of fame but through her they came to believe in what was possible. It was not stunts or tricks; it was something deeper. It was the inkling that a life which once seemed predetermined could sprout into something unimaginable. It was knowing that behind every girl's dream were past generations of women who may not have ever considered what their own dreams were. But the women of the past stood behind them both in time and in spirit, carrying them on their shoulders, ready to show up at any moment. The seed that was planted was the seed of impossibility. A seed that when planted in the right girl's heart, would blossom in such a way as to prove that anything was possible.

Afterword

I chose to end the book at the same place Reba chose to end her incredible career. This was at the height of her fame, when in her words, she *walked away from it all*. Although her story was not over at that point.

I searched to great ends to find out what her life was like after she left the circus. Many details emerged. Many of these were private, and certainly not a part of her public persona. I will sum up some points which shed light on the last decades of her life while leaving out much of what seemed quite private and was never intended for the public.

Reba moved away from Kolkata for a brief period, possibly to Delhi. There are different accounts as to why, but she had one child during this period. After a brief time away, she moved back to Kolkata. She worked several jobs, one of which was teaching yoga at Ballygunge Cultural Centre alongside Monotosh Choudhury. Later in her life, she lived alone at 52A Ballygunge Circular Road.

By all accounts, she was incredibly generous, caring and well liked. She organized neighbourhood pujas and was a follower of Sai Baba.

As was common for many girls of that era, no clear record was kept as to exactly when she was born. However, she passed away on 29 September 2010 at Ruby General Hospital in Kolkata.

Acknowledgements

I would never have started, or perhaps finished, this project without Chandrima Pal. We started this adventure together and all of her work, ideas, anecdotes and faith in the project have contributed more than I could have imagined. Much appreciated.

I am grateful to Swapan Talukdar for generously sharing about his aunty Reba.

Thank you to Monotosh Choudhury who told me about his time under Ghosh's tutelage and working side by side with Reba. I only wish his desire to visit the US would have come true. To Mukul Dutta who also shared so much.

I am grateful to Manimekhala Maiti for searching the Peary Charan Girls' School records to find Reba and Jyotsna.

Many thanks to Jerome Armstrong who, years ago, asked, 'Do you want to come to India?' This changed the course of my life completely. It was also Jerome who nudged me to write this book.

Thanks to my friends in Kolkata: Reeswav Chatterjee who helped me immensely, sometimes wandering around north Kolkata for hours in the hot sun. Arup Sen Gupta, the all-knower of the city. Muktamala and Shantanu Mitra, we have worked together for years now. Rupen for the friendship and generous sharing of history.

Thanks to John Stevens for the Bangla lessons, week by week, year by year. A big thank you to Sue Tygielski who introduced me to a few elephants—including a baby who inspired the one in this story—and shared some of her vast knowledge of the incredible animal.

I am grateful to Sumit Das Gupta of AllCap who stayed the course on this project for a handful of years. Thanks to the publisher Ajay Mago and his talented team: Chief Editor Shantanu Ray Chaudhuri for seeing merit in the book, Senior Editor Jyotsna Mehta for expertly editing the book and Sheena Agarwal for designing the wonderful cover.

Special thanks to MV Sankaran, the publishers of *Kamalasundari,* Kumar Shankar Narayan, Krishna De Ray, Sunanda Bose, Aurobindo Das Gupta, Aritra Basu, Chitralekha Shalom, Chhabi Biswas, Dipankar Gupta, Sanchita Bhattacharyya, the Centre for Studies in Social Sciences in Kolkata and Robert Miles at the British Library.

Thank you to my mom, Brigid, for more than I can put into words.

Finally, thank you to Scott who has never ceased to support me and my (sometimes unreasonably) big ideas. This project is only one small example of the many things that would not exist without you.